Fort William Henry

ILLUSTRATED

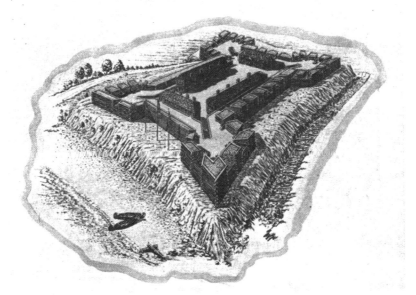

Digging up History

By Gerald E. Bradfield

Edited by Stan Werner

*" A hundred times every day I remind myself
that my inner and outer self depend on the labors
of other men, living and dead, and that I must
exert myself in order to give in the same measure
as I have received. "*

Albert Einstein

*The slightest erudition gained from the effort put forth in this
writing is dedicated to Edwin "Babe" McEnaney, whose vision
at the time of my birth created a legacy of cherished family
memories, and a wonderful life in the Adirondack region.*

Cover Design: Author

Cover Graphics

Front Cover: Tim Cordell   *"Northeast of the Fort"*

Rear Cover: The late Jack Binder   *"Southwest Bastion"*

About the Author

On a lost, but hardly forgotten sultry afternoon in the summer of 1960, an eight year old boy with a fishing pole made his way along the old railroad tracks, a journey which he knew carried with it the reward of ice cold milk and a serving of the world's most special blueberry pie. His curious destination was a little brown house seated near a thick wood of tall pines on the outskirts of the Lake George Battleground State Park. This was the house of Edwin J. McEnaney, co-founder of the Fort William Henry Corporation, and his wife Agnes, whose vivacious manner and well known culinary delights made her loved by everyone who knew her. The little boy was grandnephew Gerald (Gerry) Bradfield, who has many cherished childhood memories of "Uncle Babe" and "Aunt Aggie."

Each summer the McEnaney house was a bustling nucleus of family activity. Because of its unique location, the children and grandchildren of the family spent many hours playing in and around Fort George Park and Fort William Henry. As for the adults, conversations varying from family lineage, history, politics, and local matters usually beguiled the evening hours, exchanged over a friendly game of cards and refreshments of iced tea and lemonade. Mr. McEnaney was always fascinated by the historical significance of Lake George, and in a matter of coincidence, his wife's mother, Ellen Brown, was at one time employed as a cook in the James Fenimore Cooper House, where she recalled the familiar author being known as "Daddy Cooper." It was from these roots that young Gerald's keen interest in regional 18th century history developed.

Over the years, Gerry has served in various capacities at Fort William Henry, beginning with parking lot attendant at age fourteen. During his High School and College years he was employed as a tour guide, and was personally acquainted with the late James McGee, local historian, and the late Jack Binder, famous cartoonist, both of whom were early curators of the fort museum, and his anecdotal knowledge of these years makes an interesting addition to traditional 18th century history found in many contemporary textbooks. Following his discharge from the military in 1976, Gerald returned to the Lake George area where he and his family have lived happily for the past twenty four years. Today he occupies the position of Museum Curator.

Over the years, Gerald has spent innumerable hours on Lake George, and there is hardly a manuscript pertaining to its 18th century history with which he is not familiar. He is personally acquainted with a number of local authors and has helped to oversee four years of archaeological activity at the fort conducted by Dr. David Starbuck, local archaeologist and author of *"The Great Warpath."* Having experienced nearly fifty years of life in the Adirondacks and having been a part of Fort William Henry's continuing history, Gerald wanted to make a contribution. This book is the result.

Foreword

The average visitor discovering Lake George for the first time stands
in awe at the overwhelming beauty of the site, for all about is a
splendid mixture of nature's harmony with the hubbub of tourists
and families enjoying their well earned opportunity to reconnect with each
other and the natural beauty of the Adirondack mountains. Little does one
realize that beneath the crystal waters of the legendary lake are scattered the
archaeological remains of a war long forgotten, and the thickly forested
mountains which embrace and rise above the "Queen of American Lakes",
once echoed with the war whoops and musket fire of one of the most con-
tentious and bloody chapters of North American history.

In this spellbinding new narrative on Fort William Henry, author
Gerald Bradfield, retells for us the unforgettable story of British soldiers,
their Iroquois allies and colonial militiamen, many still in their teens,
whose 1755 victory at the Battle of Lake George and seizure of the strategic headwaters on the frontier of New France began a two year drama
which culminated in the tragic massacre immortalized in James Fenimore
Cooper's "Last of the Mohicans"

The story of the log hewn fortress in the wilderness has been carefully revealed from colonial diaries, maps and documents so vital to the
work of the historian. But the true uniqueness of today's reconstructed fort
and extensive museum, comes from the painstaking work of the archaeol-

ogist, whose trowel, hand brush and probe, for more than a generation in our own time, has unearthed the often tragic flesh and blood stories of real people, whose courageous defense of their way of life under the most primitive conditions may well be the reason that this narrative is written in English rather than French today.

In the ambition and diplomacy of Sir William Johnson, the wisdom of Mohawk Chief Hendrick, the misfortune of the dying Baron Dieskau, the nobility of French General Montcalm, as well as the hopes and aspirations of thousands of soldiers, Native Americans and farm boys turned citizen soldiers, can be seen as more than the triumph of one European empire over another, but the sowing of the seeds of a confident new nation, whose future leaders would recognize the vulnerability of their colonial overseers through trial and combat, and the realization of what they themselves had the vision to create; the independent American republic which has been the wonder of the world.

John J. McEneny
Member of Assembly, N.Y.State

Guide-historian Ft. Wm.Henry
1962-65

Acknowledgements

I would like first to express my sincere gratitude to Fort William Henry corporation president Robert Flacke Sr. for choosing me to author a book about the little log fort made famous by James Fenimore Cooper. I would also like to thank those people with whom I have enjoyed a most favorable collaboration, whose many hours of enterprising scrutiny in matters concerning our past should not go unrecognized. These dedicated people have focused not only on achieving a better understanding of our heritage through science and research, but ensuring its preservation for future generations through awareness and conservation. Without their cooperation, this book would not have been possible.

Of first mention is Dr. David Starbuck, who for many years has headed up an archaeological field school offered through Adirondack Community College. This dedicated group of students and volunteers has just completed four consecutive seasons of archaeological research at the Fort William Henry site, and working with them has been a sincere pleasure. I would also like to thank Dr. Brenda Baker from the Department of Anthropology at Arizona State University, and Dr. Maria Liston, Osteoarchaeologist at the University of Waterloo, for their extensive scientific contributions with respect to the human remains found on the property. Working with Brenda and Maria has also been a pleasure.

Not enough can be said for the crew chiefs and lab personell who documented even the most diminutive clues emerging from their respective dig sites. For those efforts I am grateful to Matt Rozell, Andy Farry, Susan Winchell-Sweeney, John Farrell, Herman "Charlie" Brown, John Kosec, and Merle Parsons.

I must also mention Dr. Russell Bellico, professor and author of several books including *"Chronicles of Lake George, Journeys in War and Peace."* Dr. Bellico and archaeologist Joe Zarzynski form the backbone of an underwater archaeological preservation group known as "Batteaux Below" and have been very much a part of the overall research effort at Fort William Henry.

Additional research assistance was provided by Frank Schlamp, adjunct archaeologist at Fort Ticonderoga, and Marie Ellsworth, Lake George Librarian, who has always offered to share her expertise regarding a number of historical projects at Fort William Henry.

With respect to the book itself, I owe a debt of gratitude to Stan Werner, freelance writer and local area tour guide. Stan's editing and proof-reading expertise was extremely helpful in the making of this manuscript. I am also thankful to Rich Parker from the Fort William Henry graphic arts department for the technical guidance he provided regarding the final assembly of the book.

The total number of site volunteers is too large to make individual recognition practical, but I would like to express my general appreciation to all those who shared in the toilsome endeavor of hauling thousands of buckets from the pit to the sifter during the course of the past four years. Their mutually cooperative effort will be reflected in museum exhibits at Fort William Henry for years to come.

The Author

♣TABLE OF ILLUSTRATIONS♣

♣TABLE OF ILLUSTRATIONS♣

CONTENTS

Prologue

Looking out over the northeast bastion of Fort William Henry, it is almost impossible to describe the natural beauty of Lake George. Just a casual glance from the shore of this lake is not enough. One must navigate its entire length to fully realize the magnetism of this ice-age legacy. Almost directly north, and roughly fourteen miles distant , the outline of Tongue Mountain can be distinguished, along with Shelving Rock, the precarious cliff from which the legendary character , *"Uncas,"* was thrown to his death in James Fenimore Cooper's *"Last of the Mohicans."* Other mountains dress the shores of the lake for its entire length, lofty and imposing, gently rising from the water's edge in some places, and forming abrupt, jagged cliffs in others. Silvery whitecaps splash upon rocky shores, as the deep, blue channel tumbles freely in the wake of an almost perpetual breeze. Whether by water or by land, the setting is one of endless panoramic beauty, inspiring the term, "Queen of American Lakes." Father Isaac Jogues, a Jesuit priest who was one of the earliest Europeans to lay eyes on this crystal clear gem of beauty, named the lake "St. Sacrement." Ironically, this beautiful wilderness valley would be better remembered in later years as the "Warpath of Nations," with Fort William Henry playing a major role in its historical essence.

It has been nearly 50 years since the first archaeological work at Fort William Henry was undertaken by Stanley M. Gifford. During that two year period Mr. Gifford contributed much to the way we interpret the events that took place at this historic site. Thousands of artifacts, both historic and pre-historic were unearthed, researched, and put on exhibit for public viewing. Human remains were discovered almost everywhere, some having been given a proper burial; others found hastily buried in cellars or otherwise scattered about. Although many of the archaeological methods used during the 1950's are considered obsolete by today's standards, the Gifford era will always be significant. In the overall scheme of things, the past half century has itself become another page in "the history" of Fort William Henry.

Contemporary authors have written a number of fine books and research papers on the subject of Fort William Henry, but in many cases an almost overwhelming sense of "number crunching" is conveyed to the reader. For the thousands of hours spent researching the subject, it is still not known exactly how many musket balls were fired, how many African Americans served at the Fort, how many perished during the massacre, and so on. In all probability, specific information of this nature will never be known. One common denominator has been established: that being an element of "exaggeration" apparent in more than a few military reports, padded inventories, journals, diaries, and other 18th century documents pertaining to the French and Indian War. Exaggeration of fact during these times was used not only as a propaganda tool, but as an effective vehicle for personal gain. With respect to written accounts of famous "massacre," exaggeration can be characterized as the manifestation of psychological aftershock, governed in measure by the individual tolerance levels of those who were exposed to scenes of unimaginable horror and barbarity. With this fact in mind, it is reasonable to assume that in an overall sense, the magnitude of the events occurring at Fort William Henry during the 18th century was proportionately less than that contained not only in original recordings, but in many contemporary writings. Cooper's literary classic is not an exception. Archaeological findings up to the present time tend to support this assumption.

Without imagination, history would be no more than a timetable, devoid of any human emotion, separated only by dates and geographic boundaries. Tangible items have proven to be healthy stimulants in this respect. The actual "feel" of an artifact such as a musket ball or a prehistoric projectile point has left some quite vivid impressions in the minds of some visitors who have passed through the fort. Many of these tourists have gone on to become active in their own local historical associations and library programs.

Whether historic or prehistoric, artifacts not only make the history book more interesting, they always provide that little bit of room for the reader to exercise the ever important element of imagination. The following pages contain excerpts from some of the finest source material available pertaining to the subject of Fort William Henry. The author has arranged these excerpts chronologicaly, in such a way that the story of the fort is told whenever possible through the writings of those who lived through various episodes, as opposed to a third party sequential narration of events. Aside from their historical significance, these passages also convey subtle human elements of wit, bravado, sarcasm, and bigotry, reminding us in an almost sobering way that these were real people, with real, very difficult lives. Some of these passages were written by the highly educated, while others were written by the barely literate. Both attempted to convey their daily observations of a harsh wartime environment from their own perspectives.

Recent archaelogical work over the past five years has added new dimension to previous research on Fort William Henry's past. State of the art computer hardware, improved research methodology, and technical advances in the field of pathology have given us a more detailed picture of life and death at this once almost forgotten frontier fort known as Fort William Henry.

Gerald E. "Gerry" Bradfield

Chapter 1

Early Regional Habitation

The James Fenimore Cooper classic, *"Last of the Mohicans"* has had tremendous influence on Fort William Henry's historical image for nearly two centuries. If not for American literature, the saga of this 18th century log fort may well have been forever lost in total obscurity. Cooper's novel focuses on the most dramatic moments of the Fort's two year existence during the 18th century, but the ground upon which the Fort William Henry was built first appears on the chronological timeline back during the glacial period, prior to the advance of the Labrador ice sheet. During that era, two rivers drained the valley of present day Lake George, with the massive shoulder of Tongue mountain and the islands in the Narrows separating the two. This area of the narrows was at one time a solid land mass connecting Tongue mountain to the eastern shore of the lake. One of the rivers originated in the trench occupied by Northwest Bay brook and flowed almost directly south into the southern basin of Lake George. This river was joined by smaller ones that rose on the high ground at Bolton and Lake George Village. The combined waters escaped from the highlands through the gap between Pilot Knob and French Mountain, eventually draining into the present day Hudson River. This escape route was responsible for the formation of Glen Lake, Round Pond, and the wetlands on the east side of French Mountain reaching southward from Kattskill Bay. The second river collected the drainage of the valley from the Narrows northward, escaping through the gap at the western base of Bald Mountain, the legendary rock from which Capt. Robert Rogers is said to have escaped from a band of pursuing Indians. Now partially filled with accumulations left by the continental ice sheet, this general area is occupied by "Rogers Rock Campsites," a State owned facility at the north end of Lake George. The waters from this river emptied into what is now Lake Champlain.

The Glacial period, therefore, was responsible for the formatioin of our present day lake. The ice sheet pushed through the valley from the north and advanced southward with sufficient mass to completely cover the tops of the bordering mountains. When the ice began its final retreat with the change of climate, the natural dividing point at Tongue Mountain was worn away, leaving the islands in the Narrows, and the river outlets both north and south were blocked with loose glacial accumulations, as the waters produced by the retreating ice contained large amounts of sediment in the form of clay, sand, and rounded boulders. A perfect example of this glacial activity is a natural stone dam which is visable in a small harbor at the lake's northern extremity. The shallow bays at both ends of the lake are lined with fine sand, making each of them a swimmer's paradise. Likewise, the waters along the eastern shore of Dome Island have tricked many an angler into thinking he has hooked the "big one," only to discover that he had hooked a chunk of the soft clay which lines the bottom of that deep water channel. Around the south end of the lake are extensive sand and gravel deposits, the most famous of which is the "promontory" overlooking the southern end of the Lake where Fort William Henry was built in 1755. This was the rather lengthy birth of Lake George, at first an extremely massive body of water. The word "promontory" was used by 18th century soldiers to describe the Fort William Henry site.

Given the geological history of the area, there was little doubt that some evidence of Aboriginal habitation of the Lake George area would be discovered when archaeologist Stanley Gifford began the first excavations at the Fort William Henry site in 1952. Little did Mr. Gifford know at the time of this undertaking that the prehistoric component of the total artifact mix would be so rich, and span such a vast period of time.

Artifacts such as pottery fragments, knives, and projectile points were discovered as deep as 12 feet below the Northwest bastion of the Fort, deep within the glacial deposit, along with several prehistoric fire

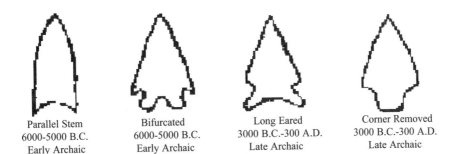

Parallel Stem	Bifurcated	Long Eared	Corner Removed
6000-5000 B.C.	6000-5000 B.C.	3000 B.C.-300 A.D.	3000 B.C.-300 A.D.
Early Archaic	Early Archaic	Late Archaic	Late Archaic

pits. A very large number of Lamoka points, after which the Lamoka complex was named, made up a large portion of this component. These points are from the Early Archaic period (8,000 B.C.-1,000 B.C.), and have radio carbon dates ranging from 3500 B.C. to 2500 B.C. The Lamoka people were indirect descendents of a widespread cultural complex of hunting and gathering societies known as Paleo-Indian. The earliest Paleo Indians inhabited North and Central America approximately 12,000 years ago, coming from Asia by way of a land bridge connecting Alaska with Siberia, and migrating south of the massive continental ice sheet that covered most of New York at that time. They were big game hunters who lived on the banks of streams and waterways in small bands of 30 or 40 people, or perhaps family units. However by the beginning of the Archaic Period, as the ice sheet began to retreat with the change of climate, many large species such as the mastodon and caribou either vanished or became extinct. As a result, these hunters

Projectile point with bifurcated base.

became more dependent on small game, wild vegetation and aquatic life as their basic source of food. Sedentary technologies such as agriculture

3

and pottery manufacture had not yet evolved, so tools from the Early Archaic period were basicly limited to hammerstones, projectile points, knives, and scrapers made from flint and various other forms of metamorphic rock, specifically quartz and quartzite. The large number of artifacts discovered from this time period during the Gifford era suggests that small groups of these people camped here repeatedly over an extended period of time.

Quartzite knife from Woodland Period

The results of archaeological work done in October of 1995 are in agreement with this line of reasoning, supported by the discovery of several bifurcate base points dating back some 5000 years. Subsequent archaeological work done in 1998 under the direction of Dr. David Starbuck brings us  to the Woodland Period (1,000 B.C - 1,200 A.D.). Excavations along the outer portion of the east wall of the fort produced a large roasting platform

Pottery Sherds from the Woodland Period.

made of stones, most of which had been fire cracked, along with a variety of pre-historic artifacts including pottery. The roasting platform itself was probably used for drying meat or fish, placing it under the catagory of food preparation, as opposed to food storage. It is not especially unique, as similar platforms have been found in other parts of New York State. Pottery sherds scattered through the charcoal of these cooking features suggest a strong link to the Owasco Culture of the Late Woodland era. Excavations at the Fort William Henry site in 1995 also produced artifacts from this time

Prehistoric Roasting Platform.

period. 74 ceramic pottery sherds from eight different vessels were discovered exhibiting Early and Late Woodland characteristics.

These discoveries and others suggest an Aboriginal occupation of this area spanning several thousand years, from the Early Archaic period through the Late Colonial Period, although there is little evidence of European occupation until about the middle of the eighteenth century. Early French explorers undoubtedly camped on the site, and Father Isaac Jogues, a Jesuit Priest from France passed through the area en route to establish a mission in the Mohawk Valley. Impressed by its beauty and crystal clear water, Father Jogues named the lake "St. Sacrament." But until Col. William Johnson arrived in 1755 and began construction of Fort William Henry, there are no written records of European occupation here.

To make an interesting speculation, the discovery of prehistoric artifacts must have aroused the curiosity of the English soldiers and Provincials in 1755, as it is highly probable that a significant number of prehistoric tools and pottery were unearthed during the construction of the original fort. The great Benjamin Franklin, commenting on the subject of anthropology, once made the remark, "...man is but a tool making animal...."

Chapter 2

The Arrival of Europeans

Generally speaking, the Owasco culture and the Point Peninsula culture were the two remaining Native American cultures to inhabit the New York area before we find any cultural traces of the Iroquois. Present day knowledge of Iroquoian origins here is obscure. Older theories of Iroquoian migration up the Ohio River, across the Detroit River into Ontario, and down into New York are no longer accepted, inasmuch as there are no traces of Iroquoian cultural remains in the Ohio Valley. The origin of the Iroquois culture in New York is still the subject of debate among anthropologists. Research indicates that the when Samuel de Champlain invaded the Mohawk Valley in 1615, the population of the entire Five Nations was probably no more than 5,500, living in small communities in the mountains throughout the central part of the State.

Similar questions linger concerning the origin of the Huron nation of western Canada. In 1639, the Jesuits compiled a list showing thirty two Huron villages and hamlets, with seven hundred dwellings, about four thousand families, and twelve thousand adult persons equaling a total population of at least twenty thousand. Yet just two centuries after the Hurons

vanished from their ancient seats, the settlers of this region stood per-
plexed over the relics of a lost people.♣

" *In the damp shadow of what seems a virgin forest, the axe and
plough bring strange secrets to light. Huge pits, close packed with skeletons and disjointed bones mixed with weapons, copper kettles, beads,
and trinkets. Not even the straggling Algonquins, who ponder the scene of
Huron prosperity can tell their origin. '*[1]

The precise origins of these nations notwithstanding, the first
Europeans to arrive in North America found the New York area to be
inhabited by Indian peoples of two distinctly different linguistic stocks.
The northern tribes spoke the Algonkin language, while the tribes further
south spoke in the tongue of the Iroquois, or Five Nations.

Prior to European arrival, the inland lake areas of Champlain and
Lake George had served for many years as an inter-tribal Indian warpath.
The French arrived in 1603, six years before the Dutch settled New York.
Upon their arrival, they discovered the Adirondacks (called by the French
Algonkins) to be at war with the Five Nations (called by the French Les
Iroquois).♣♣ The term "Five Nations" denotes a confederacy of the
Mohawk, Oneida, Onondaga, Cayuga, and Seneca tribes. This union has
continued so long that even Christians have no record of its origin. It is
likely, however, that the union at first consisted of three nations, as the
Oneidas acknowledge the Mohawks to be their Fathers, and the Cayugas
recognize the Senecas to be theirs.[2] In any event, the conflict between the
Algonkins and the Five Nations is said to have evolved in the following
way.

The Algonkins inhabited the northern part of Canada and prided
themselves as great hunters, while the Five Nations engaged themselves in
planting corn. They lived in harmony for a period of time, exchanging

---

♣ The ancient name for these people is Wendat (Oendat). The tribe was made up of twelve
smaller tribes who inhabited the region near Lake Huron. Although bitter enemies with the Five
Nations, the Hurons curiously spoke in the tongue of the Iroquois, despite being surrounded by
tribal populations of primarily Algonkin dialect.

♣♣ The reference to "Adirondacks" here is to the Indian tribe called by that name.

corn for venison. The Algonkins, however, thought themseleves to be more gallant than the Five Nations, a situation which evolved into a deadly complex of cultural esteem and hatred. It would not be long before Europeans were involved on both sides of this conflict.

Over an extended interval of time as game was becoming scarce in traditional territorial hunting grounds, the Algonkins asked if some of the young men from the Five Nations could assist them in their hunt by increasing the number of hunting parties. The Five Nations was eager to oblige in hopes of acquiring hunting skills. On this particular occasion, the Algonkins had bad luck on their hunt and were forced to return to camp. Not finding there those from the Five Nations, the Algonkins assumed they had died from hunger. Through perseverence however, the Five Nations had sustained themselves on the roots and the bark of trees. A short time later the Five Nations arrived at the camp loaded with the flesh of wild cows. This insulted and infuriated the Algonkins, but nevertheless the Five Nations were welcomed and congratulated on their success. The best meat was offered as a gift to the Algonkins, and all sat down and feasted together. Later that night the Algonkins, overcome with jealousy, murdered the Five Nations' hunting party as they slept, and returned to their people with the abundance of meat from the Five Nations' hunting party, claiming it to be theirs.

The following excerpt describes a similar event.

"Late in the Autumn of 1641, a band of Algonquins set forth on their winter hunt, and, fearful of the Iroquois, made their way northward into the depths of the forests that border the Ottowa. Here they thought themselves safe, built their lodges, and began to hunt moose and beaver. But a large party of their enemies, with a persistent ferocity that is truly astonishing, had penetrated even here, found the traces of the snow shoes, followed up their human prey, and hid at nightfall among the rocks and thickets around the encampment. At midnight, thier yells and the blows of their war clubs awakened their sleeping victims. In a few minutes, all were in their power. They bound the prisoners hand and foot, rekindled the fire, slung the kettles, cut the bodies of the slain into pieces, and boiled and devoured them before the eyes of the wretched survivors.'[3]

This was typical of the inter-tribal conflict taking place in this part of North America at the time of early European contact. And while these bloody confrontations between the two Indian nations intensified, the French had arrived and begun to settle in Canada. When the Five Nations had forced the Algonkins to retire towards Quebec, the French supported their new allies, the Algonkins, without first exploring the underlying cause of the conflict between the Algonkins and the Five Nations. Instead they formed a trading alliance not only with the Algonkins, but also with the Huron and Abenaki tribes to the west. These allies all agreed to attack the Five Nations in their own country. The earliest of these attacks occurred on Lake Champlain in a dispute over rightful ownership of the Lake George region.

For centuries, Lake George was known to the Five Nations as Andia-ta-rocte, meaning "lake that shuts itself in." [4] According to traditional tribal boundaries, these waters were well within the limits of Iroquois domination. However, when Samuel de Champlain first came upon Corlars Lake, which today bears his name, he claimed not only that

The Discovery of Lake Champlain.

lake, but all of the waters in its drainage basin in the name of France. Andia-ta-rocte empties its waters into Lake Champlain and was therefore considered a tributary body of water.

The Five Nations were unmercifully defeated by Champlain and his Indian allies in the subsequent battle for this territory, a lopsided battle in

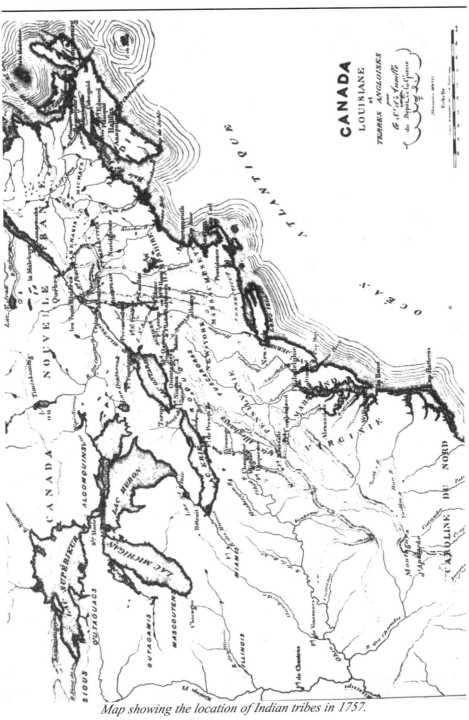

Map showing the location of Indian tribes in 1757.

11

which the Iroquois lacked firearms. The memory of this bloody debacle remained etched in the minds of the Iroquois, sparking an unbridled hatred of the French by the Five Nations. This hatred would eventually lead to numerous attacks on the Five Nations throughout the Mohawk Valley by French and Indian raiding parties. Since the English colonies were beginning to grow in population, many of the victims of these raids included innocent English settlers and their families. These attacks have been characterized as

"...a weary detail of the murder of one, two, three or more men, women or children , waylaid in the fields, woods and lonely roads, or surprised in solitary cabins. "[5]

Perhaps the most famous of these raids was the bloody night time raid on Schenectady in 1690. Sixty men, women and children were tomahawked and scalped as they lay sleeping in a town guarded only by two snowmen which the children had built on both sides of the gate. Dogs and cattle were also butchered and scalped, and the town was left a smoldering ruins. Twenty seven prisoners were also carried off to Canada that gruesome night. In reference to the attack, an Albany newspaper quoted the mayor of Albany as stating..... *"Ye women big with child, ripped up and down and ye children alive thrown into flames and their heads dashed in pieces against doors and windows."* [6] The Schenectady massacre marked the beginning of the entire 70 year conflict in North America, commonly referred to as the French and Indian Wars.

[1] The Jesuits in North America   Francis Parkman   Pg. 10

[2] The History of the Five Nations   Colden   Pg. xvii

[3] The Jesuits in North America   Francis Parkman   Pg. 342

[4] New York State Historical Association   Volume XX   Pg. 31

[5] The French and Indian Wars   F. P. Russell   Pg. 51

[6] Relief is Greatly Wanted   Edward J. Dodge   Pg. 8

Chapter 3

Why the French and Indian Wars?

In order to fully understand the role played by Fort William Henry during the French and Indian War, it is important to examine specific events, both in Europe and North America which lead up to the conflict.♣

In Europe, the Spaniards, the Dutch, the French, and the English all wanted a share in the New World. Spain had focused on Florida and Mexico, but wearied with battlefield losses and economic turmoil, Spain had difficulty sustaining further advances in North America. By the 1680's, Spain held Florida, France occupied Canada, and England possessed a chain of colonies along the Atlantic seaboard from New England to the Carolinas. Previous Dutch holdings in this area fell to the English during the Anglo-Dutch wars.

By the beginning of the 18th century Great Britain and France were essentially the only rivals in the quest for domination in North America. In Europe, four consecutive wars were waged between England and France

---

♣ The term French and Indian War is sometimes used in reference to a series of wars which made up the entire seventy year conflict.

13

to maintain a balance of power, preventing any single country from domi-
nating the Continent. These were called the War of the Grand Alliance
(1689-1697), the War of the Spanish Succession (1701-1714), the War of
the Austrian Succession (1740-1748), and the War of the Great Empire
(1754-1763). Here in the colonies, these wars were known as King
William's War, Queen Anne's War, and King George's War. The fourth
struggle between the two nations was called the French and Indian War
(1754-1763). Now the term French and Indian War is generally used to
describe the entire seventy year conflict. This last French and Indian War
was of native origin, having been waged on American soil for over a year
before legal declaration was announced in Europe. These European wars
were fought as if they were games, governed by an absurd assortment of
unyielding rules. For example, nobody fought during inclement weather,
and a stubborn General could not surrender a fortress unless its walls had
been breached sufficiently to drive a gun carriage through. Soldiers
dressed in uniforms bright enough to be seen from another planet. They
marched relentlessly toward one another in open fields, firing and reload-
ing in desperately predictable fashion. This "Gentlemen's" style of warfare was practiced throughout 18th century Europe, but even the most
experienced European General would find it of little value on the North
American frontier. Ambushed in the Ohio valley, General Edward
Braddock's army was annihilated and Braddock himself lost his life due to
European reluctance to adapt to the wilderness style warfare practiced by
the Indians and Colonials in North America.

While the kings and generals who waged these wars may have been
gentlemen, the soldiers who fought in them were not. Most were criminals
and farm boys impressed into service against their will, and drilled to the
point where they would march directly into the face of any adversity without fear. Despite repeated bloody setbacks during which thousands of soldiers lost their lives, the British continued to employ this European style
of warfare through the end of the Revolution. Even today this reluctance
to change is sufficient cause to examine the perceptibly narrow boundaries
of the 18th century British military intellectual horizon.

Both England and France had arrived in North America at the
beginning of the 17th century. France claimed the Lake George area
through discovery, while England based its claims for the area on a series
tenuous treaties with the Iroquois Nation. Territorial boundaries at this

time were also influenced by agreements between the Iroquois and Algonkin Nations which were respected centuries before the arrival of Europeans.

The alliances established between the French and the Algonkin Nation, and likewise between the English and the Iroquois Nation were almost inevitable. Differences in religious beliefs and opposing ways of life naturally divided the two European nations, and the deep seated rivalries of the Indian tribes seemed to form a complementary interlace with those of the Europeans. Inter tribal wars were intensified by the introduction of arms to the Indians through trade. When the French attacked the Iroquois at Champlain in 1615, the Iroquois apparently had never before seen firearms. This can be assumed from the following passage. *"...upon the French firing, three Captains were killed. This surpriz'd the Five Nations, for they knew that their Captains had a kind of Cuirass made of pieces of wood joined together that was proof against arrows, and they could not perceive the manner the wound was given by which they fell so suddenly...."*[1]

In addition to firearms, the Indians now had needs for other European items such as knives, axes, iron pots, and unfortunately, brandy or rum.♣ By the time the first French settlers arrived in Acadia, the Indians of that region were already addicted to alcohol, and French Brandy became the only article of trade with which the French could compete with the English and Dutch, who were able to sell most other wares cheaper.[2]

The motives of the two European nations regarding the Indians were quite opposite. The French had come to trade furs and other goods with the Indians and convert them. They saw the Indians as the middlemen of trade whose dexterity in trapping and processing pelts could ultimately result in huge profits. Goods for one livre in France could be traded to Indians for skins worth 200 livres when brought back to Paris. As a result, traders sought the skins of deer, otter, fox, and beaver, the demand for which was governed by prevailing clothing trends back in Europe.

Recognizing the potential of the Great Lakes region, the Ohio, and the Mississippi valleys, the French set up trading posts and negotiated commercial and military alliances with the Hurons, Ottawas, Illinois and

---

♣ These items were manufactured by Europeans for trade with the Indians. Thus the names "Trade Axe," "Trade Knife," "Trade Kettle," and so on.

other tribes. Intermarriage was not only permitted, but encouraged. The French actually envisioned a New World Empire, and they knew that strategic alliances with the Indians was crucial to acheiving it.

The English, on the other hand were not interested in building a new empire, but escaping an oppressive one. Although some were traders, most had established themselves as fishermen along the eastern seaboard who viewed the Indians as nothing more than a nuisance, a miserable lot of savages responsible for every misfortune on the east coast.

By the middle of the Eighteenth century there were almost one million Englishmen on the East coast compared to barely 80,000 Frenchmen in all of Canada. This disparity raises the question of why the English had not been able drive the French out of North America almost at will. The answer lies in the fact that the French operated under the unity of one authoritarian government. The English had 13 separate colonies established by different groups of colonists over an extended period of time. They were still very much fragmented.

In an atmosphere of insufferable selfishness, they often quarreled among themselves and seldom fully cooperated for a common gain. For example, a Virginan farmer cared little about Indian raids in the Mohawk Valley in which innocent women and children were butchered, or about bloody scalpings along the New Jersey border. The French and Indian War was the catalyst that ultimately brought the colonies together.

All of the colonies engaged in fur trading to some degree, but trading was concentrated most heavily in the areas of Pennsylvania and New York. The Hudson and Mohawk rivers provided easy transport of furs from Lake Erie to posts at both Albany and New York. French domination of the fur trade was now compromised by New

16

York traders in alliance with the Iroquois Nation. The resulting competition was just another factor leading to the French and Indian War

The European wars for the most part ended indecisively. By 1712, both France and Spain, weary from battlefield encounters with the British, once again desired peace. The Treaty of Utrecht, signed in 1713, resulted in a period of peace lasting 26 years, during which both England and France continued their North American expansion even though the boundary line between Canada and the British colonies remained undefined. By 1731, the French had established a base at Crown Point where Fort St. Frederic was later built. This was the place from which raiding parties were continually attacking the New England frontier. It was also the place where the French issued a bounty which significantly heightened peril to the English scalp. Perhaps due to this French decree, the Seneca chief, "Cornplanter," who lived one hundred years later, mistakenly believed that the French had taught scalping to the Indians.

In addition to Fort St.Frederic, the French also held the strategic fortress of Louisbourg on Cape Breton Island at the southern entrance to the St. Lawrence River. Louisbourg would fall to the British during the war of the 1740's, only to be given back to France in the Treaty of Aix-la-Chapelle, effectively ending King George's War.

The terms of this treaty were again indecisive with respect to North America, as no finite boundary had yet been established between England and France in the New World. The Ohio Country would now become the focus of this ongoing colonial rivalry, an area claimed by both countries but which neither country occupied. The French had begun moving into the area in force, and they had built Fort Duquesne at the forks of the Ohio river. When young George Washington led a group of Virginia militia to investigate the activities of the French in this area in 1754, his army was outnumbered and Washington was forced to surrender at Fort Necessity, a hastily built rectangular fort designed to protect the colonial army during this encounter. With Washington's defeat, the French effectively controlled the Ohio Valley.

---

[1]The History of the Five Nations   Cadwallader Colden
[2]Handbook of North American Indian   William Sturtevant
Vol. 15, Pg.83

Chapter 4

The British Plan of Attack

The treaty signed at Aix-la-Chapelle in 1748, ending King George's War, lasted approximately six years. And despite the fact that England and France had once again made peace in Europe, colonial rivalries with the French and Indians persisted in North America. These wars would continue for an entire year before theWar of the Great Empire was legally announced in Europe in May, 1756. Not only had the French established their presence in the Ohio valley, but reinforcements were being sent to Quebec, Louisbourg, and Crown Point. French and Indian raiding attacks against the New England Colonies were becoming more frequent, and the French were busily engaged in building a new fort, "Carillon," at Ticonderoga.

This aggressive activity by the French caused alarm throughout the colonies and in England. The British government, realizing that the colonies alone would be unable to prevent further French advance into the Ohio valley, placed General Edward Braddock in command of His Majesty's Forces in North America. Braddock seemed best suited for this position, inasmuch as he was nearly sixty years old with forty five years of military service. He had extensive knowledge of military affairs in Europe, and the conviction one might expect from a proud English General.

18

In a letter to Benjamin Franklin, General Braddock once wrote, *"These Savages may, indeed be a formidable enemy to your raw, American militia, but upon the King's regular and disciplined troops, Sir, it is impossible they should make any impression."* [1]

The one major flaw in General Braddock was his contempt for the Provincial Army, the Indians, and anyone else who deviated in the slightest manner from strict European Military rules. This made it difficult to secure and retain allies who would otherwise be willing to march with him. In Braddock's march to the Ohio valley, such an ally might have been Capt. Jack, the black hunter who one day returned to his cabin to discover it burned to the ground and his family murdered by Indians. Vowing undying vengence, *"he raised a band of kindred spirits, dressed and painted like Indians, and became the scourge of the red man and the champion of the white. But he and his wild crew, as useful as they might have been, shocked Braddock's sense of military fitness, and he received them so coldly that they left him."* [2]

This kind of narrow minded stubbornness would eventually be the cause of Braddock's demise. Braddock arrived in January, 1755 with two regiments of Irish regulars, the 44th and the 48th regiments of foot. After conferring with the Governors of several colonies, he and the governors agreed upon a four phase campaign. In the first, two thousand Provincials commanded by John Winslow would attack Acadia and then Louisbourg. The second, to be commanded by Braddock himself, was to capture Fort Duquesne and then attack Fort Niagara. Governor Shirley of Massachussets was to march to Oswego and launch attacks against Frontenac and Niagara. The fourth phase of the campaign would be commanded by Col. William Johnson who would attack Fort St. Frederic at Crown Point, the base from which French and Indian raiding parties were threatening all of New England.

During the first phase of the campaign, Winslow was successful in capturing Acadia, but was unable to continue on to Louisbourg due to failure of the British fleet to arrive with reinforcements. Instead he evacuated the illiterate peasant population of approximately 6,000 and burned their houses and barns. The fragmented population of Acadians re-settled in Louisiana, but a number of them eventually made it back to Acadia during times of peace. About a century later the event would become the theme for Henry Wadsworth Longfellow's poem, *"Evangeline."*

Map depicting Braddock's route

On a twelve foot wide road woven through the dense forests of western Pennsylvania, over two thousand British soldiers, Provincials, and Women were marching to their doom. Braddock's army, described as *"a thin, long parti-colored snake, red, blue and brown, trailing slowly through the depth of the leaves,"* was ambushed by a party of approximately 300 French traders and 600 Indians about ten miles outside Fort Duquesne on July 9, 1755. Over 800 enlisted men were killed or wounded, as were some

60 officers. The accompanying women were stripped, tortured, and scalped.

In describing the confusion of the English retreat, Col. George Washington wrote, *"They dashed across, helter-skelter, plunging through the water to the farther bank, leaving wounded comrades, cannon, baggage, the military chest, and the General's papers as prey to the Indians."* **3** And to the dismay of the British, the General's papers included the entire four phases of the British campaign.

Braddock's ignorance, and his unwillingness to take the advice of young Col. Washington led to the disaster. Before he died several days later, General Braddock admitted to Washington, *"had I been governed by your advice, we never should have come to this.....who would have thought it?"* **4**

Governor Shirley of Massachusetts took command of the expedition against Niagara. His army was mustered and outfitted at Schenectady, but upon hearing the news of Braddock's defeat, a large number of men deserted while the army was en-route to Oswego.

" General Shirley experienced such delays that he did not reach Oswego til the 21st of August. on his arrival, he made all necessary preparations for the expedition against Niagra, but through the desertion of batteaux men, the scarcity of wagons on the Mohawk river, and the desertion of sledge men at the carrying place, the conveyance of provisions and stores was so much retarded that nearly four weeks elapsed brfore he could go upon action. A council of war, which he held at his camp on the 18th of September, advising to the attempt on Niagra, 600 Regulars were drafted for that expedition, the artillery and ordnancewere shipped on board the sloop Ontario, and part of the provisions were put on board another sloop, the residue being ready for the row-galleys, whaleboats and batteaux. A continuation of heavy rains, which set in on the 18th, rendered it impossible for the troops (400 of whom were to go in open boats) to pass the lake with any safety until the 26th of the month, when, on the abatement of the storm, orders were immediately issued for their embarkation. These orders could not be executed. Though there was a short intermission of rain, the western winds began to blow with increased fury, and were succeeded by continual rains for 13 days. Sickness now prevailed in the camp. The few Indians that had remained had dispersed. The season was far advanced. In a council of war called on the 27th, composed of the same members who

composed the last, it was unanimously resolved advisable to defer the expedition to the succeeding year, to leave Colonel Mercer at Oswego, with a garrison of 700 men, to build two additional forts for the security of the place, and that the general should return with the rest of the army to Albany.[5]

Faced with a manpower shortage and the approaching Autumn storms characteristic of the Great Lakes area, Shirley's army was forced to remain at Oswego, and the expeditions against Forts Frontenac and Niagra never got underway. Due to the above reasons, phase three of the British scheme had failed.

The final phase of the campaign, commanded by Col. William Johnson, would be the only successful action of British arms in North America in 1755.

---

[1] The French and Indian Wars   Francis P. Russell   Ref. Pg. 94

[2] Montcalm and Wolfe   Francis Parkman

[3] Montcalm and Wolfe   Francis Parkman   Ref. Pg. 129

[4] The French and Indian Wars   Francis P. Russell   Ref. Pg. 99

[5] The History of the State of New York   A. K. White   Ref. Pg. 158

Chapter 5

The Battle of Lake George

Following Braddock's defeat in the Ohio country, it was quite apparent that the British would need a strong alliance with the Iroquois
if they were to succeed in their campaign against the French in
North America.   Because of his influence with the Indians, Col. William
Johnson was appointed Superintendant of Indian Affairs in 1755 by King
George II. Had it not been for Johnson and his Mohawk allies, the chances
of English survival in the wilderness against the French and Indians would
have been slim.

Johnson, an astute young man of Irish descent, came to America to
manage his uncle's properties in the Mohawk valley. The Iroquois knew
him as "Warraghiyagey,"   meaning "Man of many tasks."   Johnson's
treatment of the Indians was not unlike the ways of the French. He traded
fairly with them and treated them with respect. The acrid smell of bear
grease and Indian tobacco was persistent in Johnson's home as he listened

Sir William Johnson

to the interminable concerns of the Iroquois sachems.♣ And not only was Johnson respected and trusted by the Indians, he was adopted into the Mohawk tribe. After the death of his first wife he married a Mohawk princess named Caroline, the neice of his wise Mohawk friend, King Hendrick. Caroline later became known as "brown Lady Johnson."

Johnson's orders were to march to the Great Carrying Place at the upper end of the Hudson River, where a fur trading post had been established by Col. Nicholson in 1709. Here he was to erect a fortified storehouse. However, when he arrived there work had already been undertaken by a group of New Hampshire troops under a zealous Captain Robert Rogers, whose name would one day become synonymous with the legendary "Rogers Rangers." Col. Phineas Lyman then took over and completed the construction, and the fort was named Fort Lyman. Later this fort would be renamed Fort Edward in honor of a grandson of King George II.

Two logical routes of travel lay between Fort Ticonderoga and Fort Lyman, either of which could have been employed by the English to launch an attack against the French. The first was the military road inland (which was not yet completed) covering the 16 miles to the southern shore of Lake St. Sacrement, and then by water to Ticonderoga at the head of the lake. The second was by way of Wood Creek, which connects to South

---

♣ Sachems were wise Indian leaders.

Chief King Hendrick

Bay of Lake Champlain (This route closely follows that of present day Rte.4). Johnson chose to go by way of Lake St. Sacrement.

The army of about 3,000 cautiously embarked northward leaving a small contingent behind to protect Fort Lyman. When he arrived at Lake St. Sacrement Johnson wrote,

"I am building a fort at this lake which the French call Lake St. Sacrement, but I have given it the name of Lake George, not only in honor of his majesty, but to assert his undoubted dominion here. I have found it a mere wilderness not one foot cleared. I have made a good wagon road to it from Albany, distance about seventy miles; never was house or fort erected here before; we have cleared land enough to encamp men. "[1]

The army now consisted of 2,800 provincial soldiers and some 200 Indians. Col Ephram Williams was ordered to draw up plans for a four bastioned fort. Construction was delayed, however, as Johnson's Indian scouts reported seeing a large body of men in the vicinity of Wood Creek heading south toward Fort Lyman. Johnson promptly dispatched a messenger named Adams to warn Col. Blanchard at Fort Edward. Another council was called, and a plan was conceived to send 1,000 troops south on the military road either to engage the French party in the field or ensure that the line of communication between Lake George and Fort Lyman was clear. Old King Hendrick, Johnson's friend and Chief of the Mohawk Warriors was not happy with the plan and in his native tongue said to Johnson, *"If they are to die they are too many; if they are to fight, they are too few."*

The following morning one thousand soldiers led by Col. Ephram Williams, along with 200 Mohawks under King Hendrick set out on the military road to Fort Lyman. The opposing French troops were under the command of Barron Dieskau, an accomplished soldier who was

The Battle of Lake George

commissioned by Louis XV, King of France, to command the French forces in North America. Barron Dieskau was aware of Johnson's plan from the papers found on Braddock's body after his defeat. An English prisoner had informed Dieskau that Fort Lyman was weakly held and falsely reported the bulk of Johnson's army had gone back to Albany.

Armed with this incorrect information and 3,500 troops, Dieskau aggressively moved southward by way of South Bay and Wood Creek. Having left troops at Crown Point, Ticonderoga, and South Bay, he was now left with a party of only 1,500 to engage Johnson and Fort Lyman.

Dieskau's party was near the military road to Lake George about three miles from Fort Lyman when Johnson's messenger, Adams, was shot and killed by Dieskau's Indians. The letter intended for Col. Blanchard at Fort Lyman was taken to Dieskau. Two wagon drivers who had deserted the English camp were also captured and interrogated. Contrary to the story fabricated by the first English prisoner, they reported a very strong defense at Fort Lyman and a large force encamped at Lake George.

When the French party arrived at Fort Lyman, they were amazed to see a very strong fortification, well equipped and armed with heavy artillery. The Indians, generally fearful of cannon fire, refused to participate in an attack. Furthermore, many of these Indians were Iroquois who had sided with the French, but were reluctant to fight an enemy of which their own brothers were a part. This infuriated Dieskau, who then called a Council of War, and an alternative decision to attack the unfortified forces at Lake St. Sacrement was made.

Dieskau's army moved northward on the rough military road through the ravine leading to Lake George. As the army approached their destination, Indian scouts brought in an English prisoner who informed them that a party of English troops would soon be approaching. The French quickly prepared to lay an ambush. The Canadians and Indians fanned out into the surrounding woods and took their places behind boulders and trees, while the French regulars remained in the road as a "bait" for Col. Williams' men to attack.

About eight o'clock 200 Indians, led by Old King Hendrick, set out to scout ahead of the main body of troops, led by Col. Ephram Williams. The entire party had traveled about two miles down the military road when they were ordered to halt and regroup, allowing Col. Whiting's rear guard to pull up and close the gap. Almost immediately a shot rang out from the bushes. It has been cited that the first warning shot was fired by a Canadian Iroquois who recognized his cousin among Johnson's Mohawks.

"Whence came you?" called the Indian to King Hendrick.

"From the Mohawks" was his reply. *"Whence came you?"*

"From Montreal" replied the Indian.

Within seconds the entire ravine exploded with musket fire. The general confusion was multiplied by the Indians who, before firing, were constantly calling out to those attacking them to determine whether they

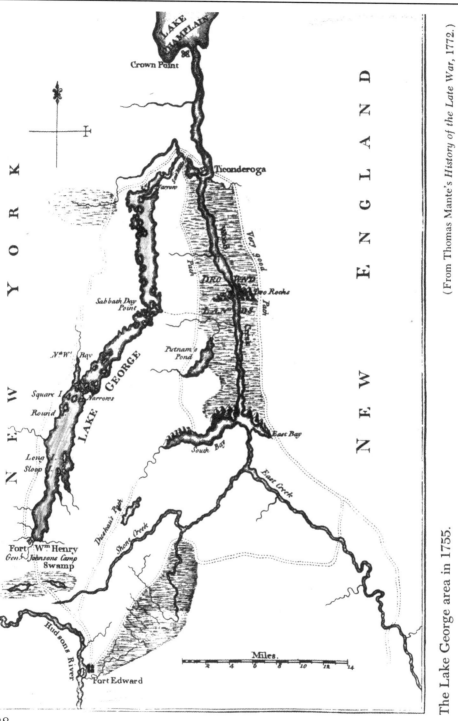

(From Thomas Mante's *History of the Late War*, 1772.)

The Lake George area in 1755.

were their own relatives from the Mohawk village of Cahghnawaga.

Both King Hendrick and Col. Williams had their horses shot from under them. Before the brave King Hendrick could separate himself from his horse, a French bayonet was plunged through his heart. Col. Williams climbed on to a rock, summoning his men to move forward, but was struck by a "ball through the brain" and killed instantly.

The remainder of the colonial troops began to retreat under the cover of Col. Whiting's rear guard. They fought from behind trees and rocks, slowly retreating toward Johnson's encampment at the southern shore of the lake, where the sound of the musket fire was getting closer almost by the minute. Makeshift walls were hastily erected from overturned wagons, bateaux, and felled trees. Artillery pieces were drawn up and loaded with grapeshot. The colonial troops now rushed toward the crude fortification that had been erected, where they were able to briefly rest and recover.

" And a very handsome retreat they made... the enemy, they were seen to drop like pidgeons. "[2]

Johnson's green army of "farmers and farmer's sons" had just dealt a major blow to the French and their Indian allies in a battle that has since been referred to as "Bloody Morning Scout." The fighting however, was far from over.

At this point, Dieskau's Indians were scattered about the woods and completely uncontrollable. Their commander, Legardeur de Saint-Pierre, had been killed in the battle. Dieskau, in the meantime was desperately trying to rally his troops and resume the attack against the English.

After considerable effort, he was able to re-assemble his troops, but without any great order. *The Canadians and Indians, helter-skelter, the woods full of them, came running with undaunted courage right down the hill upon us, expecting us to flee. Some of the men grew uneasy; while the chief officers, sword in hand, threatened instant death to any who should stir from their posts. '*[3]

The French regulars moved forward, but when they came within range, Captain Eyre opened fire with the artillery from the English encampment, forcing the military to break ranks and head for cover in the woods. *"The hailstones from heaven were never much thicker than their bullets came, but, blessed by God! that did not in the least daunt or disturb us. '*[4] Williams' men charged at the remainder of the French army,

29

and in short time the entire party of French, Canadians and Indians began to flee southward. This ended the second phase of the infamous battle.

By now the fleeing Canadians and Indians had reached the site of the morning battle and began to plunder and scalp the bodies of the dead that lay almost everywhere. They had stopped to rest near a small pond near the roadside when they were surprised by a scouting party sent out from Fort Lyman by Col. Blanchard, who had heard the musket and cannonfire throughout the day. Another battle ensued, but after a short time the Canadians and Indians, weary from the previous battle, again began to flee. According to folklore, the bodies of the dead were afterwards gathered and thrown into the pond, causing the water to turn red. Although there is no written documentation to support this particular occurence, the battle itself would come to be remembered as the "Battle of Bloody Pond," the story of which has been told many times over the years. It was the final battle in a day of fighting known as "The Battle of Lake George."

Both Johnson and Dieskau had been wounded during the fighting that morning, and both men were now in Johnson's tent receiving medical attention. Johnson had been wounded only once, but Dieskau had taken three balls in the leg.

Before Dieskau was well enough to travel, several attempts were made on his life by Johnson's Indians, who were upset by the loss of King Hendrick. Johnson however, was able to calm the Indians until Dieskau could be safely escorted to Fort Lyman. The Baron was very courtious in his remarks about Johnson and his inexperienced army, saying that *"in the morning they fought like little boys, about noon like men, and in the afternoon like devils."* Complications from the wounds he received rendered Dieskau partially disabled, and he died in Paris several years later.

News of the victory at Lake George spread quickly through the Colonies and Europe, a victory for which Johnson himself claimed all the credit. So impressed was King George II, that Johnson was made an honorary member of the royal family and granted a gratuity of five thousand pounds.

The total number of French and English who were either killed, wounded, or missing after the Battle of Lake George is estimated to be over five hundred. The English not only buried their own, but a good number of French as well, to prevent them from being scalped by the Indians.

The location of this burial ground is still unknown, although a small cemetery, or portion of a larger one containing the remains of 28 individuals, was unearthed during the construction of a local business near the intersection of Birch Avenue and Rte. 9 in Lake George.

A short distance from present day Rte. 9 just south of Bloody Pond, a large stone marks the grave of Col. Ephram Williams. In 1831, a monument honoring Col. Williams was erected on the rock where he was killed. A modern day bike path weaves through the general area of the legendary battle, and the small brook which still trickles below is called "King Hendrick Brook."

---

[1]Documents Relative To The Colonial History
Of The State Of New York   Volume VI,   Pg. 997
[2]The Journals and Papers of Seth Pomeroy
[3]The Journals and Papers of Seth Pomeroy
[4]The Journals and Papers of Seth Pomeroy

Chapter 6

The Birth of Fort William Henry

"I went out this day with Command of about 400 men to bery ye Dead Bodys of those Slain in battele ye 8th Instant we Spent ye Day In the most meloncoly Peace of Busaness. Put into ye ground 136 bodies of men. we put up & brought In a grat quantity of ye French Stores gun, blankit, hatchit etc: Provisions 2 or 3 waggon Load - brought in at night ye names of ye Dead. I have not time nor rome here to mention but my Brother - Liut Daniel Pomeroy was one of ye Brave Heroick number yt fall in that Memoriable Battle which will never be forgot."[1] On the evening of Sept. 10, 1755, Seth Pomery, a Massachusets Provincial, wiped the sweat from his brow and sat down to record this a day in which the healthiest survivors had been engaged in the somber task of burying those unfortunates who had lost their lives in the battle two days earlier. It was obvious that Johnson's men needed time to recover, but it was also quite clear that with

32

winter approaching, work at the Fort resume with the utmost urgency. So urgent was the cause that Johnson raised the English Flag on Sept.10, even though the fort at this time was only about twenty five percent complete.

Immediately after order was restored in the English encampment, Johnson's bandaged army marched over the military access road armed with shovel and axe to the ground Col. Ephram Williams had cleared before his death, while Capt. William Eyre, an engineer from the 60th Regiment of Royal Americans hastily completed plans for a four bastioned fort. A sawmill was built on the eastern side of the swamp, and before long the smell of freshly cut pine and hemlock lingered in the air as the soldiers were put to work felling trees and laying the foundation of this new fort. The soldiers referred  to the promontory of land upon which the fort was built as a "mountain of sand." Before the logs were brought there, they were hauled to the mill by oxen where they were dressed and trimmed. Within two weeks the outer walls of the fort were completed and work had begun digging the underground casemate rooms. ♣

The entrenched camp had now evolved into small community. There was a small shipyard located at the southeast corner of the lake, two lime kilns, and a brick kiln. ♣♣ There was also a hospital, the exact location of which is unknown, and tents were pitched by enterprising sutlers

---

♣ Casemate rooms were underground rooms designed for the storage of provisions. They were similar to the basements of modern day structures.

♣♣ The remains of these kilns are visible today in Fort George State Park

who had come along to do business with the soldiers garrisoned at the fort.♣ Provincial soldiers were often accompanied by wives and families to frontier outposts, and it was not uncommon for prostitutes to travel alongside these military operations, although there is no specific record of the latter having been at Fort William Henry. All civilians however, made their place in the entrenched camp.

By the beginning of October, almost every available man was engaged in the task of completing work on the fort. *"We Begun this Day to build a fort for Cannon & one quarter of our army were appointed to work at it....Between Five& Six hundred men at work at the Fort. Ensign Joseph Sheldon with 8 of Capt. Hichcock's Company Came this day that had been down at the Flats all ye time left with about 14 sick."*[2] Disease was just beginning to take its toll on the garrison. With an increasing number of soldiers becoming sick, the task of completing the Fort was becoming more difficult. To make matters worse, many soldiers had refused to engage in construction work on the fort unless given extra pay, and their officers made little effort to see that orders were obeyed.. Insubordination

---

♣ Suttlers were camp followers who peddled items of daily necessity to soldiers on military expeditions.

The Four man Log Tongs

was reaching major proportions at Lake George. The Connecticut troops refused to do any duty either to work at the fort or to mount guard, unless their demands for rations were met.[3] In addition, a considerable percentage of the American provincial troops were poorly trained and clumsy in the use of firearms.

"I was not well some time this morning. There was a Man of ye Massachussetts Regt. Shot threw ye Hart and Kild in an Instant by a Gun Going off accidentally in another Tent.... one of Capt. Jeffarys Men was Whipt 50 Lashes for Sleeping on His Post."[4]

The resulting stress caused by this dilemma apparently gave Johnson a headache. *"9 men Bury'd this day Belong'd to Col. Titcomb's Regiment, there is many now in Camp yt are Sick. General Johnson is much amis with a violent Pain in his head."*[5] These difficulties notwithstanding, work on the fort continued at a fairly brisk pace.

The final courses of brick were now being laid in the underground casemate rooms, the heavy support timbers having been anchored. These rooms were designed for long term storage of perishable provisions. Two were specificly designed as powder magazines. The primary magazine was located under the northeast bastion, while a second, smaller magazine was seated underneath the northwest bastion. All of the other underground

35

areas were destined to become bomb shelters and hospitals for the sick and wounded, regardless of their original purpose.

Another less inspiring structure being built at this time was a privy, or necessary house, which extended out over the lake from the northeast bastion in the direction of the present day steamboat dock. It was connected to the fort by a long, narrow covered passage with several ports from which muskets could be fired to protect a picketed storehouse which had been built along the north curtain, the pickets spanning the distance between the northeast and northwest bastions.♣ One French excerpt describes it as a nuisance, making it nearly impossible to get close enough to set fire to the storehouse. *"... The provincials having built a storehouse close to that Curtain which faces the lake which he had very fortunately pequcted it in; and was oblidged moreover to allott 30 men for it's defence, for had it been set on fire, the whole garrison must have been consumed, This the French General was so sensible that he offered a doubloon to each man who should set fire to it, it's preservation was greatly owing to ye Gallery leading to ye necessary house over ye Lake which had been made Musqet proof with Loop holes, from hence too ye Enemy were greatly annoyed while setting fire to to ye Sloops and Chord wood all of which were near the fort and in view of this Gallery.'*6♣♣

Interestingly enough in 1958, Mr. Robert Meader had obtained a powder horn from the Libby Museum in New Hampshire. The markings on this horn also depict the picketted storhouse and gallery. He describes the horn to Curator Stanley Gifford in the following correspondence, *"...on looking over the horn again I noticed with considerable pleasure that there were several small details that I had heretofor overlooked....I note but two small sloops, I would hazard to guess that the third had not by then been built. Nestling on the shore under the lee of the northeast bastion, and seemingly connected to it by a covered passage of some sort is a picketted storehouse."* These facts could probably be used as documentation of the earliest willful pollution of Lake George by human beings.

The final wagons of sand were now being hauled up from the beach

---

♣A storehouse was built on the outside of the north wall of the fort and a large picket fence was erected to protect it.

♣♣ The word "gallery" refers to the narrow passage leading out to the necessary house.

to fill the 29 ft. gap between the inner and outer log curtain walls.♣ Six weeks had now passed, and the fort was nearly complete. At this point General Johnson named the fort "William Henry," in honor of one grand-son of King George II, and at the same time he ordered the fort known as "Fort Lyman," be re-named "Fort Edward," in honor of another grandson of the King. Provisions and artillery were now moved into the fort from the entrenched camp, and almost daily, wagons full of provisions were arriving from Fort Edward, along with more heavy artillery. The barracks buildings erected along both the north and south walls were now complete, and a dry moat was dug along the outside of both the west and south walls. This moat would later be extended around the southeast bastion where a draw bridge would provide access to the military road leading up from the shore of the lake.

Up to this point, the only adversary of the fort had been Mother Nature. On Wednesday, Oct. 18, a violent thunderstorm erupted at the southern end of the lake, forcing a scouting party in several batteaux to scurry toward the shores and head for cover. Ligtning struck one of the tall pines in the middle of the entrenched camp, and high winds caused anoth-er to come crashing down on several tents, which fortunately were not occupied at the time. *"...about 4 of ye Clock afternoon arose a vary hard Thunder Storm. Some of our people on ye Lake with battoes Lik'd to have been Cast away but Did recover, a tree Struck with Lightning yt Stood with-in about a rod of 2 or 3 tents but hurt nobody. One tree blew Down on one shelter had lik'd to have kill'd 2 or 3 men but all Escap'd of lives recvd.. Some wounds but none mortal. wonderful Interposions of Devine Providances are Dayly Passing before my eyes in ye Deliverance from Sudden Death by accidents. Surely we carry our live in our hands.'*[7]

Then again on November 18th, an earthquake caused the chimneys of the fort to topple on the roofs of the barracks. Several gun carriages were rattled, but there were no casualties and the damage was repaired within a few days time. *"I was awakened between 4 & 5 o'clock a shock of an earthquake it lasted about a minute. no rumbling, some of the loose stones fell from the chimney tops. House wrecked. The wheels of the carriages*

♣ The curtain wall was a 29 ft. thick outer wall surrounding the perimeter of the fort. It was filled with sand hauled up from the beach.

creaked in the Fort.' **8** On the next day a New Hampshire Company commanded by Robert Rogers marched in from the bitter cold to report for duty at the newly constructed fort. *"Raw cold S E wind. The Flys begin to look for winter quarters. The New Hampshire Troops arrived. There is now in the camp sick and well about 4400 including the Recruits.'* **9**

Almost immediately Johnson dispatched Capt. Rogers and some of his men as scouts to monitor French activity at the north end of the lake. The remainder of the company would stay behind and begin construction of the old Fort Well, a task that would take nearly two months to complete. The final details involving the construction of the fort were nearing completion. Those of Johnson's provincial army who were well enough to travel had already departed for Fort Edward where they were discharged and headed home to their farms and families. The rest remained feverish in their blankets until they either became well or were added to the growing list of unfortunates who were being carried to the cemetery on a daily basis. A Connecticut man suffered from hallucinations apparently induced by fever, *"One Wm Coats of Connecticut came to me in great perplexity, saying that he Saw the Devil last night & conversed with him. He could feel the Devil in him.'* **10** With the New Year approaching, this was the miserable state of affairs at Fort William Henry which was now left with a garrison of about 350 men under the command of Col. Thatcher.

During the year 1756, no major battles were fought at Fort William Henry, and fighting was limited to skirmishes between scouting parties sent out by the opposing commanders. Not only did the garrison at Fort William Henry lack discipline and military order, sanitation concerns were practically non-existent. To exacerbate the matter, an epidemic of smallpox raged throughout the state, leaving many soldiers dead and others dying. Perhaps the best way to describe conditions at the fort during this time is through the following letter written by Lt. Col. Burton to the Earl of Loudon dated August 27th, 1756:

"My Lord,

I am got back to this place, upon my return from Fort William Henry, I take the liberty of sending your lordship a few remarks that I have made, which I shall be able to Explain to your Lordship, at my return with the Report of the State of the two Forts.

At Fort William Henry, about 2,500 men, 500 of them sick, the greatest part of them what they call poorly, they bury from five to eight daily, and officers in proportion, Extremely indolent and dirty, to a degree.

The Fort stinks enough to cause infection, they have all their sick in it, their Camp nastier than anything I could conceive, their Neccessary Houses, Kitchens, Graves and places for slaughtering cattle, all mix through their Encampment, a great waste of Provisions, the men having just what they please, no great Command kept up, Col. Gridley governs the General, not in the least alert, only one advanced Guard of a Subaltern and 24 men, no advanced pickett, no Scouting Party out from thence, when I came there, nor did they send one during my stay, which was six days.

The Cannon and Stores in great Confusion. An Intrenchment ordered and traced out by Mr. Montressor, but I am afraid will not be got done as the People are extremely indolent, and want to be brushed up by their Commanders. A great deal to be done at the Fort, more I am afraid than will be finished in time. As your Lordship will see by the report. Not near so much ground cleared of wood about the Fort as ought to be, and might have been with the peopole they have there.

They have two small sloops of about Twenty Tons each, have four swivels mounted on each, one Sloop of Thirty Tons launched the 23rd Instant, another of the same sixe to be launched in a few days, they propose having in each of those vessels, Four small Cannon or Royals. Two large Scows, and one building, a good many whaleboats, and more building. A great many Batteaus, scattered about, no guard on board the vessels, and they lay at Anchor a good way off from the Fort, that I think it would not be difficult, or any great risque to the Enemy cutting them away or burning them.

No care taken of the whaleboats, anyone making use of them that pleases, I went down to the Lake as far as the Islands, about five miles and a half from the Fort, the Lake so far about a mile over, very high hills on both sides, but highest to the Eastward, I went over to Sir William Johnson's Encampment, around the abattis and place of action, very stony and broken, but strong ground, they must have fought or run into the

39

Lake. '**11**

The Rangers, disgusted with the unsanitary living conditions within the fort itself, set up their own camp outside the east wall of the fort. This move was only one event in a plan that seemed to be changed or modified as the need arose. It also explains why features like storage buildings and sheds may appear on some original drawings of the Fort and may not appear on others, depending on the date of the particular drawing. This is partially due to a series of modifications ordered by the Royal Inspectors, who scrutinized the Fort and the surrounding area in the summer of 1756. The following is a copy of their report.

"A Report of the present State of Fort William Henry persuent to his Excelly, the Earl of Loudon's instructions to us for examining into the State of that Fort with regard to the Artillery and Military stores and the Magazines for Ammunition and provisions, and to give the Necessary Orders to prepare Barracks for the Reception and Accomodation of such a Garrison, as we shall judge necessary for the Defence of the Fort. Together with Store Houses for provisions for nine months for the Garrison Dated at the Head Quarters at Albany.

Augt. 25th, 1756

1st The Fort itself is not finished, one side being so low that the Interior is seen into (in Revers) from the rising ground on the South East side, also the East Bastion has the same defect from the grounds from the West, both of them considerably higher than the Fort, the Ditches being dug in loose sand Crumbles away so that they are at present almost without form, the Gateway and communication into the Fort is seen into from the South East, the Platforms for Cannon are Deficient, and the Salient angles are too low, no drawbridge, a bad Gate and too many Embrasures in the North West Curtine, which renders it weak. The outwork intended to scour the swamp is not finished. Its Communication, also the Ditch and Palisades are wanting without Banquetts or Platforms, or the Gorge secur'd.♣

2ndly The Casemate under the East Curtine exceeding Damp, the Timber

---

♣ This outwork was accessed by a long ditch running in a southerly direction parallel to the embankment which today runs adjacent to a local amusement park.

40

beginning to rott and all mouldy, this Casemate can contain three hundred barrells, the rest of the Casemates are somewhat better, and will contain in the whole Eleven Hundred Barrells of Provisions, the Powder Magazine is in a very bad Condition, the wet and Dampness of it, which has been the loss of One Hundred half Barrells of powder belonging to the Provincials that was stow'd there, it is capable of containing Eight Hundred Barrells.

3rdly The Barracks at present will contain Two Hundred and Twenty eight men but neither bedsteads nor bedding and no Lodgings for Officers except a few Sheds built against the North West Curtine not habitable. No Magazine for Provisions within the Fort except the Casemates just mentioned.

No Hospital, part of one of the Barracks being made for that Purpose, there is a well, the water not fit for drinking, no Guard House, the men lying in a miserable shed next the Gate. No Smith's shoop or Forge within the Fort or any place to work in.

4thly The Artillery and Stores that were there last winter, and in the Spring, according to an annex'd list, all in bad Condition, the Gun Carriages, all the Sadles and Springes are out of repair and unserviceable, there is a very small proportion of Ammunition both for the Guns and Mortars in the Fort, and the Rest of the Stores so confus'd and intermix'd that no Exact Account could be taken of them, but were oblig'd to take a return of them to the Provincial Commissary.

5th The State of the Artillery and Stores brought by the Provincials to the Camp at Fort William Henry this season will be seen by the Second list herewith Annex'd, sign'd by their Commissary, and was Examin'd into by Captain MacLeod But in regard to the Return of Shott and Shells they are found short, some being left on the road and not collected altogether.

The above being a true AND EXACT Account of the State and Condition we found Fort William Henry in, Gave the following orders and Directions for its Repairs, additional defense and necessary Buildings to be proceeded upon Immediately, according to his Lordships Instructions to us of the fore mention'd date.

1st   That the South East Curtain be raised so high with logs that the Interior part of the Fort, or its opposite Curtine may br cover'd, that the Traverese upon the East Bastion be thickened and raised with a passage underneath to go to the Bastion, that the Plaatforms be new laid and completed.

The Ditches be new Traced, with the Scarp and Counter Scarp faced with Fascines to prevent the sand Crumbling away. That a Tonaille be made in Front of the South East Curtine to Cover the Communication into the Fort, that a new Gate and Drawbridge be made, besides a bridge over the Ditch of the Tonaille.

The Salient Angles next the rising Grounds to be raised two Foot higher in order to cover better the Flanks of the Bastions, and every other Embrasure in the West Curtine to be Stop't up, the outwork next to the swamp to be finish'd with its Communications, enlarged, to move small pieces of Cannon on Occasion.

Its Gorge clos'd up with a barrier, a Ditch on its west face, and the whole Palisaded with Platforms and Banquetts.

2ndly   As the Casemates for Powder and Provisions that are bad the Tops are to be taken off, to be new Boarded and Caulk'd with a pitch Cloth over its Boarding, small Gutters to carry off the Water from penetrating into the Casemates, and air holes to keep it dry.

3rdly   It is thought Necessary that Eight Eighteen Pounders, two Thirty Pounders, Two Twelve Pounders, four Six Pounders and four Four Pounders with one Thirteen Inch Mortar, two Ten Inch Mortars be kept mounted on the Batterys of the Fort, and to Supply the outworks on Occasion with a proper proportion of Ammunition and Stores requisite for the above Number of Guns and Mortars, and also for the Infantry.

4thly   A Pile of Barracks to be built parralel to the West Curtine to Contain Two Hundred and Twenty Four men also another Pile opposite to for one Field Officer, Four Captains, Twelve Sub-alterns, One Engineeer, One Artillery Officer, as it thought necessary that this Garrison should consist of Four Hundred and Thirty Two men, Exclusive of the Ranger Company, a Hospital for Sixty men with an apartment for Surgeon and Mate, a Magazine for Nine Months provisions for Five Hundred Men, to br built parralel to the North Curtine next to the Lake on the outside of the Fort as there is not room within, this Magazine will be secured and defended by Two Flanks and Palisdes, it being out of the line of fire, it is also necessary that there should be a Small Laboratory and a Smith's Forge, with a Carpenter's Shop, a Cantine for a Suttler, an Oven for Bread, but as there is Room within the Fort for all of these Consequences, must be built in the most secure part without.

5thly   That the rising ground to the South East side of the Fort at about Seven Hundred Yards distance Caommanding the Road from Fort Edward the East Strand of the Lake and a Great part of the Swamp, a Redoubt of Block House should be erected, with a Ditch before it, mounting Two Pieces of small cannon and proper accomodation for Fifty men would Greatly Contribute to Strengthen Fort William Henry by taking possession of that advantageous piece of Ground, preventing the enemy from approaching in that way and giving timely notice to the Fort.

6thly   That the rising ground to the South West at about Four Hundred Yards distance Commands the Fort, part of the back Swamp, and the West corner of the Lake, it is a very advantagous piece of ground, if taken possession of by the Enemy for which reason. Another redoubt is propos'd on it and will be of great Security for the defence of the Fort from that side, as these two sides are most proper for an Enemy to Attack upon, and will serve as two Great Supports to the place bearing at about eight angles from one another, 'tis necessary that this redoubt should be defended and accommodated as the other, but in respect to Artillery Construction and the Force to Maintain it whenever the above redoubts are built the strength of the Garrison must be augmented fron Four Hundred and Thirty Two to Five Hundred and Thirty Two Men, with officers in proportion."

R. Burton
Lieut. Col. 48th Regt.

Jas. Montressor
Chief Engineer

Fort William Henry   *Wm. MacLord*
Aug. 25th, 1756   *Capt. Lieut. of Artillery*

43

It was not until the Major William Eyre assumed command of Fort William Henry in the Spring that a more military character would be restored, but even then, it is unclear whether all of the above recommendations were ever carried out.

[1] The Journals and Papers of Seth Pomery

[2] The Journals and Papers of Seth Pomery

[3] The Great War for the Empire   Pg. 175

[4] The Diary of Jabez Fitch   Pg. 15

[5] The Journals and Papers of Seth Pomeroy

[6] New York State Historical Society MDCCCCXXIII The Colden Papers   Pg.133

[7] The Journals and Papers of Seth Pomeroy

[8] The Diary of Rev. Samuel Chandler

[9] The Diary of Rev. Samuel Chandler

[10] The Diary of Rev. Samuel Chandler

[11] Canadian Archives Ref. 5:47   Pg. 409 - 414

Chapter 7

The Saint Patrick's Day Attack

In the Spring of 1756, Louis Joseph de Montcalm Gozon, Marquis de Montcalm arrived in Canada with the Regiment of Royal Roussilon, having been appointed Commander-in-Chief of the French armies in New France by Louis XV. Montcalm was born at the castle of Candiac near Nimes, in 1712. He was the son of Louis Daniel de Montcalm of St. Veran, and Marie Therese de Castellane-Dampus. He received a good education which he continued by private study during camp life, and at the age of nine he entered the army as an ensign. He became captain in 1729, and distinguished himself at the battles of Plaisance and Exiles. He was promoted to brigadier general in 1756 and then immediately sent to Canada.[1] The Marquis de Vaudreuil, then Governor of New France, seemed to be at odds with the bright young commander from the very beginning. Commenting on his own accomplishments, Vaudreuil never seemed to be at a loss for words. In addressing some of the Iroquois tribes who had deserted the English after the Battle of Lake George, Vaudreuil boasted, *"I have laid Oswego to ashes....the English quail before me...."*[2] He was also quick to take credit for the

45

accomplishments of Montcalm's army. Before the French victory at Oswego was known, Vaudreuil had written to the naval minister that Montcalm would not have had the courage to attack had it not been for his own inspiration and guidance. Referring to Oswego in another correspondence, Vaudreuil boasts, *"I cannot sufficiently congratulate myself on the zeal which my brother and the Canadians and Indians showed on this occasion...."*[3] Vaudreuil's brother, Pierre de Rigaud de Vaudreuil, was in command of the Canadian army. Referring to the Governor's Canadian militia, Montcalm's opinion of them was no higher than the Governor's dim view of the French regulars. Montcalm writes, *"I have used them with good effect, though not in places exposed to the enemy's fire. They know neither discipline nor subordination, and think themselves in all respects the first nation on earth."*[4]

This friction, caused mostly by Vaudreuil's jealousy of Montcalm, would result in the division of New France into two camps: one made up of Vaudreuil's Canadian provincials, and the other of Montcalm's French Regulars. Chevalier de Levis', who was an excellent diplomat, maintained communication between the two parties. An interesting parallel here is that Vaudreuil's opinion of the French regular army was not unlike Braddock's dim view of the American provincial army. But due to the efforts of de Levis', and Montcalm's detectably dry sense of humor with respect to Vaudreuil, the French were able to channel their efforts toward the more important matter of defeating the English.

Montcalm had conceived a plan to split the English colonies in half, beginning with the destruction of Fort William Henry during the summer of 1757. Upon hearing Montcalm's plan, Governor Vaudreuil once again saw an opportunity to take credit for himself, his brother, and the Canadian Militia. Having knowledge that two Irish regiments, the 44th and 48th regiments of foot, made up the better part of the fort garrison at this time, he reasoned that a surprise attack on St. Patrick's Day would be most effective. He also demanded that his younger brother, Rigaud be commander of the expedition.

On March 15, 1757 Vaudreuil's army of Canadians and Indians left Fort Carillon, marching down the ice until they arrived on the 17th at Plum Point, a point of land on the eastern shore of the lake opposite Diamond Island. Armed with some 300 scaling ladders, they approached the fort in three columns. One man at the front of each column was equipped with a pick and a lantern. These men would travel several hundred feet in front of their respective columns, periodically chopping holes in the ice to check

46

its thickness before signaling to the rest of the column that it was safe to advance. From a pre-determined distance the French army, outnumbering the English by nearly 4 to 1, was to then storm the fort and force the surrender of the garrison, which consisted of about 350 able bodied men at the time.

There are conflicting opinions about whether the garrison at the fort actually did revel in St. Patrick's Day festivities, or whether they were restrained from doing so based on the "premonitions" of their commanders. Whatever did transpire apparently had no ill-effect on the overall state of alertness in the fort. At about one o'clock in the morning on March 18th, the sentries on duty at the fort detected the sound of picks on the ice at some distance down the lake, and tiny flickers of light could be distinguished. Soon afterward the sound of footsteps could be heard, alerting the garrison that the Fort would soon be under attack. All available artillery was then drawn to the two North bastions. From then on, charges of grapeshot were fired in the direction of any sounds that were heard outside the fort, effectively keeping the Canadian-Indian army at a distance.

Vaudreuil, realizing that his element of surprise had gone awry, maintained a general assault on the fort until daybreak. That evening, the French advanced once again, but were driven back by cannon fire. On March 20, Le Mercier, chief of the Canadian Artillery, was dispatched to the fort with a message to its commander, Major William Eyre. Le Mercier was led blindfolded into the Fort, where he met with Major Eyre and the message from Rigaud was opened and read. The message proposed an immediate surrender of the fort on peaceful terms, including the Honors of War. If the offer was not accepted, then a likely general massacre by the Indians would be unpreventable.

Major Eyre promptly rejected the proposal and Le Mercier was once again blindfolded and escorted from the fort. From this point on most of the fighting took place during the hours of darkness, during which time the French burned everything combustable outside the fort. Some of the materials destroyed included several hundred bateaux, 2 ice-bound sloops, whaleboats, a sawmill, large piles of building lumber and cord wood, magazines, storehouses full of provisions, Rangers' huts, and a hospital. Mother Nature also played a role in this episode between the French and the English. The day of March 21st began with a blinding snowstorm that covered the entire area with a three foot layer of heavy wet snow, forcing Vaudreuil's army to abandon their efforts and begin the long journey back to Montreal, unsuccessful in their attempt to destroy Fort William Henry, and temper the barb of the English Lion.

The following letter Major Eyre gives a first hand account of the four day seige:

"My Lord,

Last Saturday, being the 19th instant, about one o'clock in the morning a noise of axes was heard, that seem'd to be about three miles from the Fort: And a small light was seen upon the East Side, and a very considerable way down the Lake. This gave the Alarm. Two hours or more after this, the Enemys approaches were heard very distantly upon the Ice, with their whole Army. This, we afterwards learn'd, and also that they had 300 Scaling ladders and all the apparatus necessary for a general Assault: This drew upon them a Smart fire of Artillery, and Small Arms which obliged the main Body to Retire. After this they attempted to set on Fire, one of the Sloops and the Batteaus but were prevented; other Efforts were used before daylight to accomplish this Affair, which they likewise failed in. At the Break of day the Enemy withdrew, and a few men were sent out to see what they could discover, who found a few Scaling Ladders and Several other Empliments, to set the Vessels and Boats on fire.

By Prisoners we afterwards took, we found the Enemy were very numerous; one of their Accounts is that they were 1650, another upwards of two Thousand, consisting of Regulars, Colony Troops (or their Independent Company's) Canadians and Indians.

The Enemy Soon after they disappeared began to show themselves again on the Lake, and on each side of it, and by degrees their appearance grew more Formidable; They were filing offin Large Bodys to surround us, and at the same time kept a heavy fire of small Arms upon the Garrison. The fire of our Artillery Checked their approach, and by that we could discover, made their different detatchments Retire, for they made no Attempt that they, only fired Smartly, with Musquetry, The next morning being the 20th, another Attempt was made by their whole Army, to storm the place, but by the heavy fire from the Garrison, were drove back; This happened very early; Not Succeeding they set on Fire, two Sloops, and burnt almost all our Batteaus; and when daylight appeared drew off. About mid-day their Army were seen marching across the Lake in Regular Bodys and seemed very numerous, as if returning toward Ticonderoga; but presently after a few men were seen coming towards the Fort (with a red Flag) on the Ice, who made Signals at half a miles distance to have someone sent to speak to them. I complied with this, and sent an Officer and

48

four Men, with an Other Flag to meet them; presently after one of our own people brought me a letter which was from Mons. de Vaudreuil, Commander of the French Army, a Copy of which I enclose, in Consequence of the Letter I sent an Officer to bring in Mons. le Mercier Blindfolded. The Substance of whose message I have likewise enclosed.

— I desired him to make my Compliments to His General, and tell him, my fixt Resolution was, to defend His Majesty's Garrison to the last Extremity. Upon this he was carried back blindfolded as he came, and soon after their Army were seen to move toward us, every thing in Readiness for the General Assault; and tho we were sickly, a General firmness could be discovered by the behaviour of the Troops, so as to give great hopes, they would do their Part. The Officers behaved with the greatest diligence Care and Resolution. The Enemys fire was soon Renewed, by some detatched Partys; The main Body kept at a distance. That night or Early the next morning, a third General Assault was undertaken, which they likewise failed in. They not succeeding set on Fire two Storehouses, (in one of them a good deal of Provisions) on one side; a Provincial Storehouse, and all the Rangers Hutts (within side their Picketted Fort) on the other. These different fires burnt with such Violence, so as to make one apprehend, at one side of the Fort, that the other or opposite Quarters were in Flames; Yet happily by proper care and Vigilence within side, no damage was done. In this situation we Continued the most part of the night, a perfect Silence was observed, and a Constant fire kept upon the Enemy, whenever we could make any discovery by means of the Fires, or before were made by listening with the utmost Attention. The different times that the Enemy Intended a general Assault under the cover of darkness, they were wholly baffled, by steadily keeping up to this Method, for our Eyes at these times, were of no use to us, being excessively dark.

The next day being Monday the 21st the Enemy withdrew at datbreak, in their usual way; This morning very few of their Straglers remain'd, and about nine or 10 o'Clock it began to Snow and continued the whole day and night, during which time the fire on both sides in a great measure ceased, and we could not discover that they attempt anything during that time. Tuesday the 22nd early in the morning, the Enemy seem'd Resolved to burn the Sloop up on the Stocks; Several times they were beat off, but still persevered & by means of Combustibles and dry Faggots, which they brought from their Encampment at least effected their design; during the whole tome they frequently attempted to set Fire to our Picketted

Storehouse, that is next to the Lake, but were always bravely beat off. The last Effects must have been used to preserve this place as it could not fail of Setting the Garrison in flames if they had Succeeded.♣ The Sloop upon the Stocks continued blazing until broad day on Wednesday, when we discovered a man in the Swamp Seemingly wounded; a Small party was ordered to bring him in; at which time, another of the Enemy was found behind a pile of Chord wood; which last I apprehend was afraid of going off after the Sloop was in a blaze, as no Body could move there abouts, but must have been discovered. These are the prisoners we now have; a Third was brought in, who had Scarcely life when taken to the Hospital. A little time after this the Enemy wholly disappeared.

The Whaleboats, Scows, or Gundalas & Bayboats Escaped the Conflagration. We have had only Seven Men slightly wounded. The Prisoners tell us our Artillery had good Effect.

> *I am,*
> *My Lord*
> *with great respect*
> *Your Lordship's*
> *Most Obediient*
> *Humble Servent*
> *Will: Eyre*
> *Maj. to 44th Regiment*

P.S. - I send the Intelligence and Declaration of the two Prisoners, and likewise a List of the things they inform me their Army were provided with for this Expedition.

> *Strength of the Garrison of Fort Wm. Henry*
> *When the Enemy came before it.*
> *Regulars fit for duty..............................274*
> *Rangers ditto..72*
>
> *Total well   346*
> *Sick Regulars andRangers.....................128*
>
> *Total Sick and Well   474"*

♣ The successful defense of this picketed storehouse can be greatly attributed to an aforementioned passage to a privy over the lake, which had been specificly designed to protect it. Chapter 3 contains a French reference to the structure.

The St. Patrick's day attack on Fort William Henry was a victory for both the English and the French. The English, Irish, and Provincial troops at Fort William Henry had gallantly defended the fort and forced Vaudreuil's Canadian army to retreat to Canada. Victory, however, would be sweeter for the French, as Vaudreuil's army had severely weakened the English position at the head of Lake George by destroying large numbers of military vessels, buildings, and provisions.

The miserable aftermath of Vaudreuil's raid would not only require the most efficient use of all available manpower to restore, but the work would also test the limits of even the healthiest reinforcements, the main body of which was already en-route to the Fort. At just about the time the last of Vaudreuil's Canadians and Indians were arriving back in Canada, Col. George Monro arrived at Lake George with fresh troops of the 35th, 44th, and 48th regiments of foot to assume command of Fort William Henry. Within several days Major Eyre was relieved of his command and Col. Monro would begin the ugly task of restoring military order to both the English fort and the fortified camp.

---

[1] A Historical Journal of the Campaigns in North America   Knox
[2] Montcalm and Wolfe   Ref. Pg. 271
[3] Montcalm and Wolfe   Ref. Pg. 268
[4] Montcalm and Wolfe   Ref. Pg. 270

Chapter 8

Montcalm's Attack

"We are hard at work at our Carrying place embarking our provisions, artillery. The naval engagement, the arrival of the prisoners, the joy that has spread throughout the camps, have somewhat deranged us today, for working, but at early dawn to-morrow I shall be at the Falls, and at six o'clock at your brother's camp, to review the Marine battalion, to look at the completion of our Militia brigades, to hold a Council with the Nations, and to fix the Great Council at which I am to present them in the King's name with the Large Belt you have placed in my hands.'[1]   These were the words of the Marquis de Montcalm, written in a letter to Governor Vaudreuil dated July 27, 1757. Montcalm's army at this time had assembled at Carillon and was making final preparations before proceeding down Lake George to attack Fort William Henry.   Enthusiasm abounded, but getting an army of nearly 12,000 men, provisions, cannon, batteaux, and other munitions of war to Carillon alone had been a wearisome task. Here

52

The Marquis de Montcalm.

had assembled the darkest coalition of cultural extremes, an equivocal brotherhood of soldier, volunteer, priest, and pagan. Aside from the cultural barriers around which this fragile league was woven, the expedition faced a number of other uncertainties long before the army's departure from Montreal.

The St. Patrick's Day assault against Fort William Henry having been considered a success, Governor Vaudreuil decided to follow through with Montcalm's plan to beseige both Fort William Henry and Fort Edward and gave orders to make immediate preparations. In his ordinary state of perpetual arrogance, Vaudreuil writes, *" The more important is this expedition, the more bent am I on doing my best to assure its success. For that purpose, I have placed at the disposal of the Marquis de Montcalm an army of about nine thousand men, composed of Regulars of the Line, the detatchment of Marines, Canadians and Indians, with a respectable train of artillery."* [2]

The project was jeapordized almost immediately by a shortage of provisions. *" The delay of water conveyance and want of provisions ren-*

dered this operation doubtful; as the first ships that arrived at Quebec in the end of June and in the course of July did not bring sufficient to the seige of Fort George to be undertaken...."[3] In a separate correspondence, the pompous Governor writes, *"I have had the greatest facility in organizing that army through the good disposition of the Regulars, Marines, Canadians amd Indians. The only obstacle I experienced was in victualing the army...."*[4]

Faced with this dilemma, Vaudreuil commissioned Sieur de Martel, the Inspector of the King's stores, to make a strict search in the farmers' houses for all the provisions they might possess. *"Every farmer, full of zeal for his country, voluntarily reduced himself to a very small portion, barely adequate for his support until the harvest, and whatever was over, supplied the wants of the seige."*[5]

In this manner, enough food was collected to sustain an army of 12,000 men for one month, mostly Indian corn and bacon which were somewhat resistant to perishability. During this same time emissaries for the French governor had been busy recruiting Indian tribes from the west and north, promising bountiful plunder in the form of loot and scalps. Furthermore, the news of Montcalm's victory over the English at Oswego had aroused the curiosity of these so called upper country Indians, many of whom were anxious to meet this man who *"tramples the English under his feet."*♣ Within a short time various tribes from the west and north began to arrive and camp at Montreal in anticipation of the attack on Fort William Henry. Over two thousand Indians from thirty three different nations would participate in the assault. The composition of the force is listed below.

Royal Army on Lake St. Sacrament

Marquis de Montcalm, Major General
Chevalier de Levis, Brigadier
Sieurs de Rigaud and de Bourlamaque, Colonels
Chevalier de Montreuil, Major General

♣ This was a reference to Montcalm's victory over the English at Oswego.

Regulars

La Reine----------------360)
Landuedoc ------------322)   Brigade of La Reine.
Marine------------------520)
La Sarre ---------------451)
Guyenne----------------492)   Brigade of La Sarre
Royal Rousillon- - - - 472)
Bearn - - - - - - - - - 464)   Brigade of Royal
                                 Rousillon
Total - - - - - - - - - - - - - - - - - 3,081

Militia

La Corne's Brigade - 411
Vassan's- - - - - - - - - 445
St. Ours' - - - - - - - - 461
Repentign's - - - - - - 432
Courtemanche's- - - - 473
Gaspe's - - - - - - - - - 424
Villiers' Volunteers - 300

Total - - - - - - - - - - - - - - - - - 2,946

Artillery, Sieur Mercier, Commandant.

Officers - - - - - - - - - 8
Gunners, Bombadiers 180

Engineers, Sieurs Desandrouin and de
                Lobiniere

Indians

Domiciliated- - - - - - 820
Upper Country - - - - 855
Total Army- - - - - - - - - - - - - 7,890

Deducting the sick, the non-effectiveness of the battalions the garrisons left at Carillon, the Falls, and the head of the Carrying Place, this army amounted to 5,400 fighting men exclusive of the Indians.

Special Return of the Indians

Domiciliated Indians

Nations		Officers attatched to them.
Nepissings - - - - - - - - - - - - - - - - 53		Msr's. Langris, Montegron M. de la Corne St. Luc.
Algonkins	of the Lake - - - - - -) of the Three Rivers -) 47	Abbe Matavet, Missionary M. St. Germain, Interpreter
Abenakis	of St. Francis - - - - -) of Bekancourt - - - -) 245 of Missiscoui - - - - -) of Panaouameske - -)	Chevalier de Niverville, Hertel Father Oubal, Jesuit Missionary Chateauvieux, Interpreter
Iroquois	of Sault St. Louis - -) of the Lake of 2 Mts. -) of La Presentation -) - - - - - - - - - - - - - 363 Oneidas of the Five Nations - - - - - - - -)	DeLongueil, Sabrevois Abbe Piquet, Sulpitian, Missionary Pertuis, Laforce, Interpreters
Micmacs	of Acadia - - - - - - -) 4	
Hurons	of Detroit - - - - - - -) 52 of Lorette - - - - - - -)	Chevalier de Niverville, Hertel
Amalecites	- - - - - - - - - - - - -) 56	Abbe Piquet, Sulpitian, Missionary Loniere, Interpreter

820

Indians of the Upper Countries

Tetes de Boule - 3

Outaouais,	Kiscacones - - - - - - - - - 94)	
	Sinago - - - - - - - - - - - - 35)	
	of the Forks- - - - - - - - - 70)	
	of Mignojan - - - - - - - - 10)	
	of Beaver Island- - - - - - 44)	337
	of Detroit - - - - - - - - - - 30)	
	of Saguinau- - - - - - - - - 54)	

Sauteurs	of Chagoamigon- - - - - - 33)	
	of Beaver - - - - - - - - - - 23)	
	of Coasekimagen - - - - - 14)	
	of the Carp - - - - - - - - - 37)	
	of the Cabibonke - - - - - 50)	157

Poutouatamis	of St. Joseph - - - - - - - - 70)	
	of Detroit - - - - - - - - - - 18)	88

Folles,	Avoines of Original - - - - 62)	
	of the Chat - - - - - - - - - 67)	129

Miramis- 15
Puans   of the Bay- - - - - - - - - - 48
Ayegais - 10
Foxes - 20
Ouillas - 10
Sacs - 33
Loups - 5

Total - 855

Total Indians - 1,675

The Cayugas, Senecas, and Onondagas also sided with the French, bringing the number of Indians to over two thousand. This was an early French roster of tribes and sub-tribes, some of which evolved into tribes presently known by other names.

As the list shows, each tribe had its own interpreter, and the Christian tribes had missionaries among them. After the last of the upper country Indians had arrived at Montreal, Montcalm's army moved up the St. Lawrence River to Sorel, where they were joined by Christian tribes who inhabited the outer French colonies. Here the entire congregation of Indians was assembled for the ceremonial "war song," at which Montcalm ever so gently gained the trust of his Indian allies, treating them almost like children. This ceremony was followed by a feast. On the next day, the army began the long journey down along the Richellieu river into Lake Champlain, and then on to Ticonderoga.

At about this time some of the young French officers who had never before seen any of these Indians from the upper country were beginning to take notice of their mannerisms and living habits. Montcalm's aide' de Camp, Bougainville, could not distinguish one nation from the other. *"I see no difference in the dress, ornaments, dances, and songs of these various western nations. They go naked, excepting a strip of cloth passed through a belt, and paint themselves black, red, blue, and other colors. Their heads are shaved and adorned with bunches of feathers, and they wear rings of brass wire in their ears. They wear beaver skin blankets, and carry lances, bows, and arrows, and quivers made of the skins of beasts. For the rest they are very straight, well made, and generally very tall. Their religion is brute paganism."*

Father Robaud, Jesuit missionary to the Ottawas, made his own observation. *"Imagine... a great assembly of savages adorned with every ornament most suited to disfigure them in European eyes, painted with vermilion, white, green, yellow, and black made of soot and the scrapings of pots. A single savage face combines all these different colors, methodically laid on with the help of a little tallow, which serves for pomatum. The head is shaved except at the top, where there is a small tuft, to which are fastened feathers, a few beads of wampum, or some such trinket. Every part of the head has its ornament. Pendants hang from the nose and also from the ears, which are split in infancy and drawn down by weights till they flap against the shoulders. The rest of the equipment answers to this fantastic decoration: a shirt bedaubed with vermilion, wampum, wampum collars, silver bracelets, a large knife hanging on the breast, moose-skin moccasons, and a belt of various colors always absurdly com-*

bined."[6]

Bougainville goes on to say, *"Their paradise is to be drunk...,"* referring to the number of kegs of brandy consumed, and that it was almost impossible to keep them fed. Rations for one week would be devoured in three days time.[7] By the time Montcalm's army reached the portage at the north end of Lake George, all of the artillery, batteaux, canoes, and military stores had to be hauled over the passage with brute force by the soldiers themselves, inasmuch as the beasts procured to perform this duty had all found their way to the Indian cooking pots. This dismal enlightenment was met with great disgust by at least one brigade of soldiers, ordered by Montcalm to work through the night to move the burdensome transports, and it was especially insulting to the Royal Rousillon brigade which was given further orders to complete the miserable task on the following morning. In a letter to the Minister, Bougainville describes the ordeal.

The movement of *"considerable artillery, of munitions of war, of every description, of provisions to victual the entire army for nearly a month, of 250 batteaux, of 200 canoes, could be completed only in the night of the 31st to the 1st of August. We had neither oxen nor horses. Everything was done by the men's arms, and in the last days the entire brigades, headed by their Lieutent-Colonels, relieved each other for this work as long as it was laborious."*

Due to this delay, the army was not completely assembled at the head of Lake George until nearly the end of July. The French officers did little to prevent these outrages, ever fearful that the Indians would pack up and go back to their own countries.

While Montcalm was busy making last minute preparations for the march, Colonel Monro had dispatched Colonel Parker and 350 provincial soldiers known as the "New Jersey Blues" to investigate French activity at the opposite end of the lake, and to attempt to burn the sawmill at the falls. Twenty two whaleboats departed from the southern shore during the evening of July 25th, twenty of which would never return. Shortly after

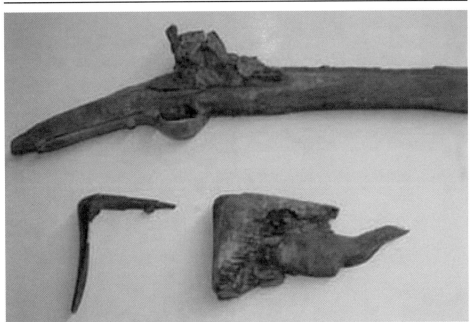

Musket and brass butt plate recovered from Lake George

Brass butt plate stamped with the words "New Jersey."

A   *NUMB. 263.*

Supplement to the *New-York Mercury.*

MONDAY, *August* 1, 1757.

NEW-YORK, *Aug.* 1. Late laft Night arrived here the Poft from Albany ; by whom we have the following

Extract of a Letter, from a Gentleman at Fort William-Henry, to his Friend in New-York.

FORT WILLIAM-HENRY, *July* 26, 1757.

SIR,

I AM forry that I have nothing better to relate to you than the following melancholly Affair, viz. Colonel John Parker, with three of his Captains, and fix or feven Subalterns, with Captain Robert Maginis, Captain Jonathan Ogden, Lieutenants Campbell and Cotes, of the New-York Regiment, with about 350 Men, went out on the 21ft Inftant, in Order to attack the advanced Guard at Ticonderoga by Water, in Whale and Bay-Boats : They landed that Night on an Ifland, and fent before Break of Day to the Main Land three Battoes, which the Enemy way-laid, and took. Thefe Battoes were to land two Miles this Side ; they being taken, gave the Enemy Intelligence of their Defign of Landing. Our Men next Morning at Day Break, made for faid Point, and the Enemy, who knew our Scheme, contrived as a Decoy, to have three Battoes making for faid Point, which our People imagining to be the three Battoes fent out the Evening before, eagerly put to the Land, where about 300 Men lay in Ambufh, and from behind the Point came out 40 or 50 Canoes, Whale and Bay Boats, which furrounded them entirely, and cut off every one that was in the Circle. Colonel Parker and Captain Ogden, are the only two Officers that have efcaped with Life, the Latter much wounded in the Head. Capt. Maginis, and every one in the Boat with him, are killed ; and not one Man left alive that were in the Bay-Boats. Captain Woodward being terribly wounded, jumped overboard, and was drown'd. Captain Shaw killed ; Lieutenants Campbell and Cotes of the New-York Regiment, they fay for certain are killed ; a Captain of the New-Jerfey Regiment is alfo killed, but have not yet learnt his Name. Upon the Whole, only Parker and Ogden efcaped, with about 70 Men, all the Remainder, being about 280, are killed, or taken.

Since the foregoing, Colonel Glazier has received a Letter from a Serjeant belonging to Captain Maginis's Company, who fays, that in the hotteft of the Fire they forced their Battoe thro' the Enemy's Line, being favoured with the Smoak and Fog, and efcaped with 6 or 7 more, that were alive with him in the Battoe, and landed on the Eaft Side, where he luckily met with Captain Weft from Fort-Edward, on a Scout ; and as every Man made the beft of his Way as foon as they landed, none but himfelf is yet come in fafe.

P. S. What could the Enemy be doing there ? They certainly were going on fome great Defign, by being there in fo large a Body, as is judged 1000 Men at leaft.

Copy of the letter which appeared in the New York Mercury on July 16, 1757

daybreak on the 26th, as the small fleet rounded the tip of Sabbath Day Point, the war whoop was heard and a band of Ottawas who had been wait-ing in ambush launched their canoes in hot pursuit. Stricken with fear and panic, some men threw away their arms and tried to swim for their lives but were either captured, or speared like fish and scalped by the Indians. Montcalm writes to Governor Vaudreuil, *"The Outaouais who arrived with me, and whom I designed to go on a scouting party towards the lake, had conceived the project of administering a corrective to the English barges, and you will see,*
Sir, that it has been administered......the whoops of our Indians impressed them with such terror, that they made out a feeble resistance; two barges only escaped, all the others were captured or sunk. I have 160 prisoners, five of whom are officers. About 160 men have been killed or drowned."[8]

The following letter appeared in the New York Mercury on August 1, 1757. It was written by an unknown gentleman who was stationed at Fort William Henry, describing the return of those who survived the Sabbath Day Point massacre. The intended recipient was a friend in New York. Some translation has been made by the author.

"Sir,

I am sorry that I have nothing better to relate to you than the following melancholly affair, viz. Colonel John Parker, with three of his Captains, and fix or Seven Subalterns, with Captain Maginis, Captain John Ogden, Lieutennants Campbell and Cotes, of the New York Regiment, with about 350 Men, went out on the 21st Instant, in Order to mark the advanced Guard at Ticonderoga by Water, in Whale and Bay boats. They landed that Night on an Island, and went before Break of Day to the Main Land three Battoes which the Enemy way-laid, and took. The fe Battoes were to land two Miles this Side; they being taken, gave the Enemy Intelligence if their Design of Landing. Our Men next Morning at Day Break, made for faid Point, and the Enemy, who knew our Scheme, contrived as a Decoy, to have Battoes making for said Point, which our People imagining to be the three Battoes fent out the Evening before, eagerly put to the Land, wher about 300 Men lay in Ambush, and from behind the Point came out 40 or 50 Canoes, Whale and Bay Boats, which surrounded them entirely, and cut off every one that was in the Circle. Colonel Parker and Captain Ogden are the only two Officers that have escaped with Life, thw Latter much wounded in the Head. Capt. Maginnis and everyone in the Boat with him; and not one Man left alive that were in the Bay Boats. Captain Woodward being terribly wounded, jumped over-

62

board and was drown'd. Captain Shaw killed; Lieutennants Campbell and Cotes of the New York Regiment, they say for certain are killed; a Captain of the New Jersey Regiment is also killed, but have not yet learnt his Name. Upon the Whole, only Parker and Ogden escaped, with about 70 Men, all the Remainder, being about 280, are killed, or taken.

Since the foregoing, Colonel Glazier has received a Letter from a Sarjent belonging to captain Maginis's Company, who says that in the hottest of the Fire they forced their Battoe thru the Enemy's Line, being favoured with the Smoke and Fog, and escaped with 6 or 7 more, that were alive with him in the Battoe, and landed on the East Side, where he luckily met with captain /west from Fort Edward, on a Scout; and as every Man made the best of his Way as soon as they landed, none but himself is yet come in safe.

P.S. What could the Enemy be doing there? They certainly were going by Some great Design, by being there in so large a Body; as is judged 1000 Men at least."

Meanwhile the Indians, intoxicated with the thrill of their victory, had become uncontrollable and wished to leave with their prisoners immediately. This gave cause for a Council to be held with the Nations in an effort to reach an agreeable compromise, one which included the improbable covenant of white bread and shoes. Montcalm also wished to communicate his plan of battle to the Chiefs of all the Nations, in order that they could confer together and express their opinions of the plan at the Grand Council fixed for the following day. *"Many of the Indians wishing to leave with their prisoners, the Marquis de Montcalm has had considerable trouble to retain them and to prevail on them to consent to send the prisoneers to Montreal, which consent they retracted in the evening; he has been obliged to issue counter orders, to dispatch one of his Aids-de-Camp, at 9 o'clock at night; to the Carrying place to hold a Council with the Chiefs of all the Nations, and to collect their opinions, who have unanimously consented to the departure of the prisoners, on condition that the Governor-General would have great care taken of them, and have white bread and shoes given them...."* [9] During this period of tempermental tribal volatility, Father Robaud was returning to the camp of the Ottawas, when he came upon a sight that goes beyond the limits of human imagination.

" My tent had been placed in the middle of the encampment of the Outouais. The first object which presented itself to my eyes on arriving there was a large fire, while the wooden spits fixed in the earth gave signs of a feast. There was indeed one taking place. But O Heaven! What a

63

feast! The remains of the body of an Englishman was there, the skin stripped off, and more than one half of the flesh gone. A moment after I perceived these human beings eat with famishing avidity of this flesh; I saw them taking up this detestable broth in large spoons, and apparently without being able to satisfy themselves with it. They informed me that they had prepared themselves for this feast by drinking from skulls filled with human blood, while their smeared faces and stained lips gave evidence to the truth of their story. "**10**

Speaking in broken French, a young Indian warrior heckled the Jesuit priest, proclaiming *"You have French taste; I have Indian. This is good meat for me."* The French soldiers again did nothing to prevent the abomination, fearful that any intervention would have caused the Ottawas to *"go home in a rage."* **11** Whatever was not consumed that evening was devoured the next morning when the noisome feast resumed. Two other English soldiers met a similar fate, whose charred vestiges lay scattered in the ashes of the Indian roasting pits. The French didn't outwardly show it, but even the most seasoned officers were unnerved by the nefarious spectacle. Bougainville writes, " *..the Indians...drawn 500 leagues by the smell of fresh human flesh and the opportunity to teach their youths how to cut up a person destined for the cooking pot. These are the comrades who are our shadow day and night. I shudder at the ghastly spectacles which they are preparing for us."* **12**

The Grand Council was called on the following evening , at which time the Nations took their respective places in ranks determined by their own tribal laws. When all was in order, Montcalm addressed them in a charismatic, soft spoken manner. *"Children, I am delighted to see you all joined in this good work. So long as you remain one, the English cannot resist you. The great King has sent me to protect and defend you; but above all he has charged me to make you happy and unconquerable, by establishing among you the union which ought to prevail among brothers, children of one father, the great Ontario......by it I bind you all together, so that none of you can separate from the rest till the English are defeated and their Fort destroyed."* He then presented them with a wampum belt of six thousand beads in the name of the King and said, *"Take this sacred pledgd of his word. The union of the beads of which it is made is the sign of your united strength. By it I bind you all together, so that none of you can separate from the rest until the English are defeated and the fort destroyed."* Nipissing chief Kikensick addressed his tribe: *"....he has bound us all together by the most solemn of ties. Let us take care that nothing shall separate us."* **13**

The other interpreters each in turn related Montcalm's message to their subsequent tribes, and soon the Council erupted with applause. According to tribal law, the right of the belt belonged to the Iroquois, who were the most numerous of the Nations present with the army. Speaking for the entire assemblage, the Iroquois volunteered themselves as guides to Chevalier de Levis', whose army of nearly two thousand was to march through the steep, rocky mountains on the western shore of the lake and arrive at the first rendezvous point, the Bay of Ganaouske (Northwest Bay).

They also agreed that one third of the Indians present should travel over land, and that those remaining should go by water. With all the Nations in agreement, a thunderous applause once again was heard, and the Council came to a close without incident. Montcalm's timing of the Council could not have been better, as Bougainville writes, *This solemn and customary act was, under existing circumstances, more important than ever. For during several days, hardly could those be retained who participated in the fight on Lake St. Sacrament (Sabbath Day Point); these people scrupling to incur again the risk of war after one success, pretending that such would be tempting the Master of Life and bringing down on them bad luck.* **14**

Having full knowledge of the difficult mountain terrain, Kanaktagon, a famous Iroquois hunter, suggested that de Levis' army embark two days ahead of the main body of the army which was traveling by water. This would facilitate a simultaneous rendezvous at Northwest Bay. Here the league would build three fires to act as a signal for the men in the first batteaux to round the shoulder of Tongue mountain.

On the morning of July 30 as the sun rose over the mountaain known as Anthony's Nose, Chevalier de Levis' detachment began its march from the Burnt Camp into the dense forests along the western shore of the lake, having been instructed by Montcalm to travel lightly equiped.
♣ *"This detachment marched in the morning from the Burnt Camp without tents, kettles, or equipage.....volunteers and some Indians forming the vanguard. The Canadians and remainder of the Indians marching as flankers, the troops in the centre, in three columns."* **15**

At this point Montcalm issued strict orders forbidding any disbursement of alcohol to the Indians. As a result, the Indians from the upper country had become not only bored, but increasingly restless with super-

---

♣ The Burnt Camp is today known as Howe's Point. It was accidentally set on fire in the weeks preceeding the assault on Fort William Henry , which accounts for its name

stition, interpreting every delay as a bad omen. *"The Indians destined to go by water, set out at night and were to wait for the army three leagues from the Portage; they were weary of their inactivity in a camp where there was neither brandy nor wine to drink. Our domiciliated Indians, in truth children of Prayer, afforded occupation to the Missionaries, to whom the day was scarcely long enough to confess them. But this pious exercise was not for the upper country Nations, whose superstions and excessively restless mind was juggling, dreaming, and fancying that every delay portended misfortune. On marching, these Nations left suspended a complete equipment as a sacrifice to the "Manitou," to render him propitious."* **16**

At two o'clock in the afternoon on August 1, Montcalm's army set sail for the southern end of Lake George in 250 batteaux, leaving behind a garrison of 100 men at Carillon, and 150 more at the portage. Within several hours the army met with the Indians who had been waiting in an area just north of Sabbath Day Point. After a brief rendezvous, the army resumed the expedition, the Indians having taken the lead in 150 bark canoes. Gliding over the tranquil waters along the western shoreline, the small fleet slowly vanished into the darkness of night.

At 3 o'clock in the morning on August 2, the army arrived at Northwest Bay and saw the three signal fires at some distance across the bay on the western shore as the first batteaux emerged from the Narrows and rounded the base of Tongue Mountain.✦ Here at the camp of deLevis' they would rest in preparation for the following day. *"At three o'clock in the morning the army arrived at Ganaouske' bay. Three fires lighted on the shore, which was the signal agreed upon, notified us that Cevalier de Levis was posted there, having arrived at four o'clock on the preceeding evening, after a march which the eccessive heats, the continual mountains, the fallen trees, the necessity of carrying everything on one's shoulders had rendered fatiguing even to the Indians...."* **17** After resting for the night, de Levis' detatchment would depart again at 10 o'clock in the morning and begin reconoitering the positions around the fort, and Montcalm would put his army in motion at noon, halting in a sandy cove on the western shore of the lake near a place called English Brook late in the evening.

Meanwhile, a scouting party in two whaleboats had set out from the fort to observe movements in this area, when, not unlike Sabbath Day Point, the war whoop was sounded and several hundred Indians launched their canoes in hot pursuit. *"The army arrived at the same cove in the*

✦ The site of present day Bolton Landing.

evening. During the night, two English barks out scouting were discovered by the Indians, who gave them chase and made three prisoners, who on being interrogated on the spot, told us that the enemy numbered 3,000 men, 500 of whom were in the fort, the remainder in the entrenched camp on a height convenient to the fort, to relieve its garrison every day; that all the troops had orders to stand to their arms, and to come to meet us on the firing of the signal gun.' **18**

On August 3, while the French artillery was still being put ashore, the first cannon shot was fired beginning an excruciating six day battle. *"At two o'clock in the morning a gun from the Fort was heard and the Abenaki scouts gave notice that all was in motion in the English camp. The Marquis de Montcalm immediately gave orders to approach the Fort and this order was repeated, to receive the enemy in case they came against us; and should they not come, to invest the place, and even to attack the intrenched camp, if it were considered susceptible of being taken by main force."* **19**

On the next day the French were engaged in digging the artillery entrenchments, during which time the Indians exchanged a brisk volley of musket fire with the fort.

"The Indians have kept up sharp fire on the fort, repelled several sorties, killed more than one hundred men, took 4 prisoners, killed a hundred beeves (cattle), *150 sheep, took 40 oxen and 20 horses."* **20** At this point Montcalm ordered fires lit to serve as beacons for the remaining artillery batteaux which had not yet arrived. Once the firing had begun, the explosions could be heard 16 miles away at Fort Edward.

"Before Sunrise We Heard ye Cannon Play Vary Brisk at ye Lake Soon after ye Small arms began to Fire this Firing Lasted all Day without Much Ceasing it was Contluded that this Day there was ye Most Ammunition Expended that Ever was in a Day at that Plais Before." **21**

Throughout the attack Col. Monro had repeatedly dispatched couriers to General Webb at Fort Edward, begging for reinforcements.Frightened himself by Montcalm's ferocity, Webb refused to send them. Furthermore, Webb's dispatches to Monro were intercepted by Montcalm's Indians. From the 5th of August forward, the sequence of events is best told by an eyewitness who was inside the Fort during the seige. The gentleman appears to be quite literate, possessing an astute knowledge of artillery, yet his name is unknown. The following excerpts have been taken from the journal of this anonymous officer who describes the next several days at the Fort as he saw them in August, 1757.

Friday 5th. *"This morning the Enemy began to cannonade our forts with nine pieces of Cannon 18 & 12 pounders. It was some Time before they could find their mark. At Eleven they tried their shells, mostly 13 inches in diameter, which fell short but towards the afternoon they got their distance very well, Several of their small shells falling into the Parade Ground. One of their shot carried away the pully of our Flag Staff and the falling of our flag. Much rejoiced the Enemy; but it was soon hoisted tho' one of the men that was doing this had his head Shot off with*

An artist's conception of the fort under siege

a ball, and another wounded. A part of the Enemy and their Indians advanced near our camp on which the brave Cap. Waldo of the N. England forces (Joseph Frye's regiment) went out to take possession of of piece of rising ground near the wood on which brisk fire ensued on both sides. Col. Monro sent out a second party to Surround the Enemy, but they were forced back and the Enemy advanced up to our quarter Guard. Capt. M. Cloud brought his cannon to bear upon them soon dispersed them. Here an unlucky accident happened, as some of our men were returning to Camp were taken for the enemy and fired upon by which several were killed and wounded. During this attack poor capt. Waldo was Shot and Soon Expired. Capt. Cunningham of the 55th Regt. was wounded in the right arm."

Saturday 6th. *"Last nigth the enemy carried their entrenchment and erected a battery of 10 Guns mostly 18 pounders about 6 or 700 yards from us bearing N. W. both of Cannon and Mortars. This was the hottest days action from all quarters; tho' as yet our garrison remained in high spirits expecting Sir William Johnson with the militia and Gen. Lyman with the N. England Forces to the number of 3 or 4000 men which we heard were on their march with some more cannon. Would to God they were permitted to come as their good will was not wanting. A party of Indians were*

An accurate portrayl of a mortar firing

Ten inch mortar, burst from overuse

seen advancing with great speed towards the road that leads to Fort
Edward which Confirmed us on our belief of relief.

About 11 o'Clock Monsr. Montcalm sent an officer with a Flag with
a letter that was intercepted by the above mentioned Indians from Gen.
Webb wrote bt his Aid-de-Camp Mr. Bartman to Col. Monro aquainting
him that his Excellency could not give him the assistance as the militia had
not come up to Fort Edward, & c. The French officer delivered another letter from Montcalm aquainting Col. Monro that he came from Europe and
Should Carry on the war as a Gentlenan and not as the Savages do but like
a true Frenchman, broke both his word and Articles of Capitulation as will
appear in the sequel of this relation. During this interval the Enemy made
a show of all their Indians, about 1200, on a rising ground about about
250 yards distance bearing S.W. while their engineers reconnoitered our
old camp ground which was afterwards a great Advantage to them. As
soon as theor officer returned they began their fire in good Earnest which
we returned with the utmost bravery. This day we split two of our heavi-
est Pieces of Cannon (vizt. 32 pounders) and our largest Mortar was rendered useless which was very unlucky for us as we could not be supplied
with others in their place. This day Col. Monro published his orders to all
in the fort that if any person proved cowardly or offered to advise giving up
the Fort that he should be immediately hanged over the walls of the Fort
and he did not doubt but the officers in the Garrison would stand by him to
the last and that he was determined to stand it out to the last or as long as

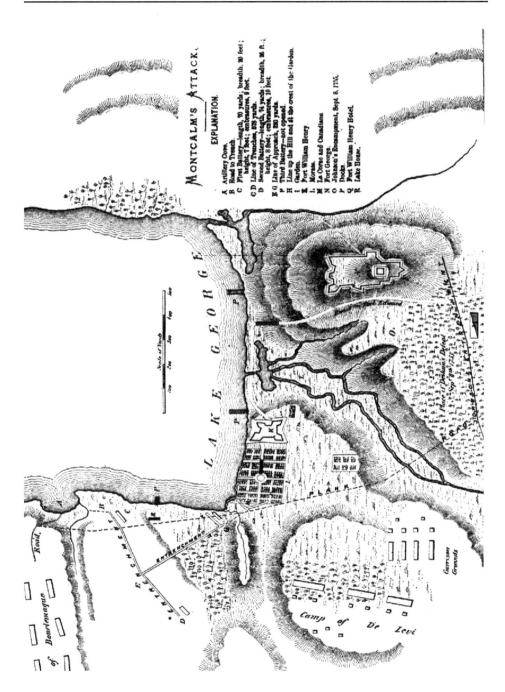

Montcalm's Plan of Attack

his two legs were together."

Sunday 7th. "*The Enemy continued playing us very hard with their Cannon and Bombs while the Compliment was returned by us with all our Artillery, still hoping for a Reinforcement from Fort Edward. A Shell fell into the South Bastion broke one man's leg and wounded another; Split one of our 18 pounders and burst a Mortar. Several of the Enemy's shells fell near the campS. S.E. of our Fort about 400 yards distance and on line with the fort from the Enemys two Batteries, so that their shot missing the Fort should Srike the Camp. It appeared that the Enemy could throw their shells 1300 yards. A shell fell amongst the Officers whilst at dinner; but did no other mischief than Spoil their dinner by the dirt it tore up. Another Shell fell into the east or Flag Bastion and wounded two or three men.*"

Monday 8th. "*We now began to believewe were much slighted, having received no reinforcement from Fort Edward as was long expected. The Enemy were continuing their Approaches with their Entrenchments from the 2nd Battery towards the Hill on our old Camp Ground, where they were erecting a third Battery, which would have greatly distressed us. There were frequently during these last 2 or 3 days smart skirmishes near our Camp, but we beat them off the Ground. This night we could hear the Enemy at work in our Garden, on which some Grape Shott was sent in amongst them, which had good Effect as it drove them off, however they got their 3rd Battery almost finished by Day Light.*"

Tuesday 9th. "*This day the Enemies Lines were finished, parallel to our West Curtain in the Garden, Distance about 150 Yards. Col. Monro, after a Council of War had been convened, wherein the Officers were of Opinion, that the loss of our heavy Cannon vizt. 2, 32pounders, 1, 24 pounder, two 18 pounders, one 9 pounder & 3 Mortars bursting would render it impossible to defend the Fort much longer, as the Enemy's Batteries had increased and our metal failing us, & no help coming, wherefore it was thought advisable that a white Flag should be hung out in order to capitulate; which was done accordingly, and the firing ceased: The Enemy very readilly granted the Capitulation: had Monsieur Montcalm been a Man of Honor, he would have performed this part; but instead of that such a Scene of Barbarity ensued as is scarce to be credited: After tht Articles were agreed on & signed, the Officers left the Fort to a Regiment of French Regulars whi were ready at the Gate, thro' which we marched with most of our valuable Effects & Arms to the entrenched Camp and in the Evening three Companies of thr 35th Regt. had marched out & the other three Companies were on their march out of the Breastwork, when we received orders to return to our Posts again where we remained till next morning."*

　　　With the exception of the sick and wounded, the garrison at this point had been escorted to the entrenched camp and had prepared for the march to Fort Edward. Montcalm, knowing all too well the indiscriminate nature of Indian barbarity, prudently postponed the march until the following morning. This precautionary measure however, would be ineffective in preventing the bloody catastrophe that was destined to occur on the following day.

---

[1] Documents Relative To The Colonial History Of The State Of New York　　Volume X, Pg. 591 - 594

[2] Documents Relative To The Colonial History Of The State Of New York　　　　Volume X Pg. 584 - 586

[3] Documents Relative To The Colonial History Of The State Of New York　　　　Volume.X Pg. 640 - 651

[4] Documents Relative To The Colonial History Of The State Of New York　　　　Volume X Pg. 584 - 586

[5] Documents Relative To The Colonial History Of The State Of New York　　　　Volume X Pg. 640 - 651

[6] Montcalm and Wolfe　　　　Parkman　　　　Pg. 280

[7] Montcalm and Wolfe　　　　Parkman　　　　Pg. 279

[8] Documents Relative To The Colonial History Of The State Of New York　　　　Volume X Pg. 591 - 594

[9] Documents Relative To The Colonial History Of The State Of New York　　　　Volume X Pg. 640 - 651

[10] The Jesuits in North America　　　　Parkman

[11] Montcalm and Wolfe　　　　Parkman　　　　Pg. 281

[12] Betrayals　　　　Steele　　　　Pg.85

[13] Montcalm and Wolfe　　　　Parkman

[14] Documents Relative To The Colonial History Of The State Of New York　　　　Volume X Pg. 605 - 618　　　　Bougainville to M. de Paulmy

[15] Documents Relative To The Colonial History Of The State Of New York　　　　Volume X Pg. 605 - 618　　　　Bougainville to M. de Paulmy

[16] Documents Relative To The Colonial History Of The State Of New York　　　　Volume X Pg. 605 - 618　　　　Bougainville to M. de Paulmy

[17] Documents Relative To The Colonial History Of The State Of New York　　　　Volume X Pg. 605 - 618　　　　Bougainville to M. de Paulmy

[18] Documents Relative To The Colonial History Of The State Of New York　　　　Volume X Pg. 605 - 618　　　　Bougainville to M. de Paulmy

[19] Documents Relative To The Colonial History Of The State Of New York　　Volume X　Pg. 605 - 618　　　　Bougainville to M. de Paulmy

[20] Documents Relative To The Colonial History Of The State Of New York　　Volume X　Pg. 592 - 605　　　　Journal of the Expedition Against Fort William Henry

[21] The Diary of Jabez Fitch Jr.　　　　Pg. 17

Chapter 9

The Massacre

It was about 11 o'clock in the morning on the day before the massacre when the garrison at the Fort marched to the French lines for the formalities of surrender. The evening before Col. Monro called a council of his officers and the terms of surrender were agreed upon. Meanwhile Montcalm, uneasy with the demeanor of the Indians at this point, would not sign the agreement until he had consulted with the Chiefs of all the Nations. A general council was called, at which time Montcalm *"explained the conditions upon which the English offered to surrender. The Chiefs unanimously assured him that they would approve whatever he would do, and that thy would prevent their young men from committing any disorder."* [1] This detail having been attended to, Montcalm agreed to the terms, and the articles of capitulation listed below would be signed by both Monro and Montcalm on the occasion of this colorful but dismal ceremony.

74

"Article 1st

>The garrison of Fort William Henry, and the troops in the intrenched camp adjoining, shall march out with arms, and other honors of war.

>The baggage of the officers and of the soldiers only.

>They shall proceed to Fort Edward escorted by a detatchment of French troops and some officers and Interpreters attatched to the Indians, and at early hour tomorrow morning.

Article 2nd

>The gate of the Fort shall be delivered up to the troops of his Most Christioan Majesty after the signing of the capitulation and the entrenched camp, on the departure of his Britanic Majesty's troops.

Article 3rd

>All the artillery, warlike stores, provisions and in general everything except the effects of the officers and soldiers specified in the first article, shall upon honor, be delivered up to the troops of His Most Christian Majesty, and with that view an extract inventory of the property herein mentioned shall be delivered after the capitulation, observing that this Article includes the fort, intrenchment, and dependencies.

Article 4th

>The garrison of the fort, intrenched camp and dependencies shall not be at liberty to serve for eighteen months, reckoning from this date, against his Most Christian Majesty, nor against his allies; and with the capitulation shall furnish an exact return of his troops, wherein shall be set forth the names of the officers, Majors, other officers, Engineers, artillery officers, Commissaries and employees.

Article 5th

>All the officers, soldiers, Canadians, women and Indians, taken on land since the commencement of this war in North America, shall be delivered at Carillon within the space of three months, on the receipts of the French Commandants, to whom they shall be at liberty to serve, according to the return which shall be given in thereof by the English offi-

cer, who will have charge of the prisoners.

Article 6th

> *An officer shall be given as a hostage until the return of the detachment, which will be furnished as an escort for his Britannic Majesty's troops.*

Article 7th

> *All the sick and wounded who are not in a condition to be removed to Fort Edward, shall remain under the protection of the Marquis de Montcalm, who will take proper care of them and return them immediately after they are cured.*

Article 8th

> *Provisions for the substinence of said troops shall be issued for this day and tomorrow only.*

Article 9th

> *The Marquis de Montcalm being willing to show Lieutenant-Colonel Monro and his garrison some token of his esteem on account of their honorable defense, grants them one piece of cannon, a six pounder.*

> *Done at noon, in the trenches before Fort William Henry, the ninth of August, Nine thousand seven hundred and fifty seven.*

(Signed) George Monro, Lieutenant- Colonel, 35th and Commandant of his Majesty's forces in and near Fort William Henry

> *Granted in the name of his Most Christian Majesty, pursuant to the power I possess from the Marquis de Vaudril, his Governor and Lieutenant General in New France*

(Signed) Montcalm"

Customary protocol having been observed, Montcalm immediately assigned a number of his own men to gather and inventory all of the

English military stores, artillery pieces, and other spoils of war.

Meanwhile, the soldiers of the fort garrison were dimly engaged in gathering whatever personal effects were allowed in accordance with the articles of capitulation, and preparing for the march to the entrenched camp. Montcalm, sensing an increasing unrest among the Indians, judiciously ordered that all stores of alcoholic beverages in the fort be shattered, an order which may, or may not have been carried out. *"After this promise had been solemnly given by all the chiefs, the capitulation was signed. In order not to omit anything that prudence dictated on like occasion, the Marquis de Montcalm had ordered Sieur de Bougainville, his Aide-de-Camp,, who was with Lieut, Colonel Monro the Commander of the fort, to have the wine, brandy, rum and all the intoxicating liquors split; to confine the troops to the entrenched camp, where they were to remain according to the capitulation, until the next day, when they were to be conducted to Fort Edward, notifying him that otherwise, 'twould not be possible to restrain that multitude of Indians."*[2]

Some time during the late afternoon of August 9th, the vanquished army of Colonials and Regulars began the gloomy procession to the entrenched camp, not only under supervision of the French guard, but under the covetous eyes of darkest depravity. Just as the last of the spiritless column stumbled across the drawbridge, the Indians entered the fort and began pillaging. They rummaged through officers' chests and other personal effects, some of which undoubtedly contained rum rations. They then entered the underground casemate rooms where the sick and wounded lay, and began to murder and scalp. Father Robaud, who was one of the first to enter the Fort after the capitulation was signed, saw a Huron emerge from one of the casmate rooms, waving in the air a human head, testimony of his uncivilized brutality. *"... I saw one of these barbarians come forth out of the casements, which nothing but the most insatiate avidity for blood would induce him to enter, for the infected atmosphere which exhaled from it was insupportable, carrying in his hand a human head, from which streams of blood were flowing, and which he paraded as the most valuable prize he had been able to seize...."* ♣

♣ During early archaeological excavations, five skeletons were unearthed from one of the cellars along the east side of the Parade ground. One of those skeletons was missing a skull.

Some of the Indians then invaded the entrenched camp, invoking more horror by sinking their tomahawks into the skulls of the sick and wounded , and scalping them in their tents. These Indians were not restrained until abut nine o'clock in the evening. *"Notwithstanding all the precautions that had been taken, the Indians, who got into the entrenchment of the English, wished to pillage their chests; the latter, opposing such proceeding. 'twas to be feared that some serious disorder would ensue. The Marquis de Montcalm ran thither immediately; prayers, threats, caresses, consultations with chiefs, interposition of the officers and interpreters, who have some authority over these savages; he made use of every means to stop and restrain them. About 9 o'clock at night he appeared to have accomplished that object."*[3]

For those gathered in the entrenched camp, never had a more restless night been spent than that of August 9th, 1757. The sinister faces of the Indians and the sight of their blood stained tomahawks had instilled in the doomed English garrison unimaginable fear, while the terror in their whoops and yells was saluted throughout the night by an unholy requiem sung by a choir of wolves. Unarmed and distressed, the English prisoners once again prepared themselves for the perilous march to Fort Edward at about 4 o'clock the next morning. Jonathan Carver, a provincial volunteer, was one who not only witnessed the massacre, but lived to tell about it. The sequence of events described by Mr. Carver is very consistent with those of other eyewitnesses. The following is Carver's recollection of the massacre.♣♣

" In consideration of the gallant defence the garrison had made, they were to be permitted to to march out with all the honours of war, to be allowed covered wagons to transport their baggage to Fort Edward, and a guard to protect them from the fury of the savages.

The morning after the capitulation was signed, and as soon as day broke, this whole garrison, now consisting of about 2000 men, besides the women and children, were drawn up within the lines, and on

♣♣ Some historians have questioned the credibility of Carver's journal because the number 1,500 is used in his reference to the number killed during the massacre. This number has been taken out of context. Carver's journal reads that 1,500 were *"either killed or taken prisoner,"* leaving the passage open to an entirely different interpretation.

the point of marching off, when great numbers of the Indians gathered about them, and began to plunder.

The troops were at first in hopes that this was their only view, and suffered them to proceed without opposition. Indeed it was not in their power to make any, had they been so inclined; for, though they were permitted to carry off their arms, yet they were not allowed a single round of ammunition.

In these hopes however they were disappointed, for presently some of the savages began to attack the sick and wounded, when such as were not able to crawl into the ranks, notwithstanding they endeavoured to avert the fury of their enemies by their shrieks and groans, were soon dispatched. (killed)

Here the troops were fully in expectation the disturbances would have ended, and the little army began to move, but in a short time they saw the front division driven back, and discovered that they were encircled by the savages.

They expected every moment that the guard, which the French by the articles of capitulation had agreed to allow them, would have arrived and put and end to their apprehensions, but none appeared. The Indians now began to strip everyone, without exception, of their arms and clothes, and those who made the least resistance felt the weight of their tomahawks.

Three or four of the savages laid hold of me, and whilst some held their weapons over my head, the others soon disrobed me of my coat, waistcoat, hat and buckles, not omitting to take from me that money which I had in my pockets. As this was transacted close by the passage that led from the lines on to the plain near which a French centinal was posted, I ran to him and claimed his protection, but the Frenchman only called me an English dog, and thrust me with violence back into the midst of the Indians.

I now endeavoured to join a body of the garrison that were crowded together at some distance, but innumerable were the strokes that were made at me with different weapons as I passed along. Luckily, however, the savages were so close together that they could not strike to hurt me without endangering each other, notwithstanding which one of them found means to make thrust at me with a spear which grazed my side, and from another I received a wound with the same kind of weapon to my ankle. At length I gained the spot where my countrymen stood, and forced myself

79

into the midst of them, but before I got thus far out of the hands of the Indians, the collar and ribbons of my shirt were all that remained of it, and my flesh was scratched and torn in many places from their savage claws.

By this time the war whoop was given, and the Indians begain to murder those that were nearest to them without distinction. It is not in the power of words to give any tolerable idea of the horrid scene that now ensued. Men, women, and children were dispatched in the most wanton and cruel manner, and immediately scalped. Many of these savages drank the blood of their victims as it flowed from their fatal wounds.

We now perceived, tho' too late to avail us, that we were to expect no relief from the French, and that, contrary to the agreement they had so lately signed to allow us a sufficient force to protect us from their barbarities, the tactily permitted them, for I could perceive the French officers walking about at a distance discoursing together with apparent unconcern.

For the honour of human nature I would hope that this flagrant breach of every sacred law proceed rather from the savage disposition of the Indians, who are almost impossible to control, then to any premeditated design in the French Commander. An unprejudiced observer would however be apt to conclude, that a body of 10,000 Christian troops must have had it in their power to prevent the massacre from becoming so general. But, whatever was the cause from which it arose, the consequences of it are dreadful, and not paralleled in modern history.

As the circle in which I stood enclosed was by this time much thinned, and death seemed to be approaching with hasty strides, it was proposed by some of the most resolute to make one vigorous effort to endeavour to make their way through the savages, the only probable method of preserving the lives of those who remained. This however desperate, was resolved on, and about 20 sprung at once into the midst of them. In a moment they were all separated, and what was the fate of my companions could not be learned till some months after, when I was informed that only six or seven of them survived. Intent on my own hazardous situation, I endeavoured to make my way through the savages in the best manner possible, and I have often been astonished since, when I have recollected with what composure I took, as I did, every necessary step for my preservation. Some I overturned, being at the time young and athletic, and others I passed by, dextrously avoiding their weapons, till at last two very stout chiefs of the most savage tribe, as I could distinguish by their

80

dress, whole strength I could not resist, laid hold of me by each arm and began to force me through the crowd.

I now resigned myself to my fate, not doubting that they intended to dispatch me, and to satiate their their vengance with my blood, as I found they were hurrying towards a retired swamp that lay at some distance. But before we got many yards, an English gentleman of some distinction, as I could tell by his breeches, the only covering he had on, which were of fine scarlet velvet, rushed by us. One of the Indians instantly relinquished his hold, and springing on this new object, endeavoured to seize him as his prey, but the gentleman, being strong, threw him to the ground, and would probably have gotten away, had not he who held my other arm quitted me to assist his brother. I seizes the opportunity, and hastened away to join another party of English troops that were yet unbroken, and stood in a body at some distance, but before I had taken many steps I hastily cast my eyes toward the gentleman, and saw the Indian's tomahawk gash his back, and heard him utter his last groan. This added to both my speed and desperation.

I had left this shocking scene but a few yards, when a fine boy about 12 years of age, that had hitherto escaped, came up to me, and begged that I would let him lay hold of me, so that he might stand some chance of getting out of the hands of the savages. I told him that I would give him every assistance in my power, and bid him lay hold, but in a few moments he was torn from my side, and by his shrieks I judged he was quickly scalped alive, I could not hellp forgetting my own situation for a moment to lament the fate of so young a sufferer, but it was utterly impossible for me to take any method to prevent it.

I now got once more into the midst of friends, but we were unable to afford each other any succour. As this was the division that had advanced furthest from the fort. I thought ther might be a possibility, though a bare one, of forcing my way throught the outer ranks of the Indians, and get into a neighboring wood. I was the more encouraged to hope by the almost miraculous preservatiion I had already experienced, nor were my hopes in vain, or the efforts I made ineffectual. Suffice it to say that I reached the wood, but by the time I had penetrated a little way into it, my breath was so exhausted that I threw myself into a brake, and lay for some minutes apparently at tje last gasp. At length I recovered the power of respiration, but my apprehensions returned with all their former force when I saw several savages pass by, probably in pursuit of me, at no

81

very great distance. In this situation I knew not whether it was better to conceal myself where I lay till night should come on. Fearing, however that they would return the same way, I thought it most prudent to get farther from the scene of of my past distresses. Accordingly, striking into another part of the wood, I hastened on as fast as the briers and the loss of one of my shoes would permit me, and after a slow progress of some hours, gained a hill that overlooked a plain that I had just left, from whence I could discern that the bloody storm still raged with unbashed fury. After passing three days without subsistence, and enduring the severity of the cold winds for three nights, I at length reached Fort Edward, where with proper care my body soon recovered it's proper strength, and my mind, as far as the recollection of of the late melancholy events would permit, its usual composure.

It is computed that 1500 persons were killed or made prisoners during this dreadful day. Many of the latter were carried off by the savages and never returned. A few, through favourable accidents, found their way back to their native country, after having experienced a long and severe captivity.

The brave Col. Monro had hastened away, soon after the carnage began, to the French camp, to endeavour to procure the guard agreed on by the stipulation, but his application proving ineffectual, he remained there till General Webb sent a party of troops to demand and protect him back to Fort Edward. But these unhappy occurances, which would probably have been prevented, had he been left to pursue his own plans, together with the loss of so many brave fellows murdered in cold blood, to whose valour he had been so lately a witness, made such an impression on his mind, that he did not long survive. He died in about three months of a broken heart, and with truth might it be said, that he was an honour to his country.

I mean not to point out the following circumstances as the immediate judgement of Heaven, and intended as an atonement for this slaughter, but I cannot omit observing that very few of these different tribes of Indians that shared in it ever lived to return home. The smallpox, by means of the communications with the Europeans, found its way among them, and made equal havok by its malignity to what they themselves had done by their brutalities. The method they pursued, in the first attack of that disorder, to abate the fever attending it, rendered it fatal while their blood was in the state of fermentation, and Nature was striving to throw

82

out the peccant matter they checked her operations by plunging into water,
the consequence was that they died by the hundreds. the few that survived
were transformed into hideous objects, and bore with them to the grave,
deep indented marks of this much dreaded disease."[4]

Mr. Carver's recollection of the massacre was obviously told a
number of years after the fact, and a modest sense of bravado is detectable
in the writing. The final paragraphs in the journal are in reference to smallpox. When the Indians plundered the Fort, they did not neglect to dig up
and loot the cemetery. Since most of those buried there had succumbed to
the fatal disease, its subsequent effect on an Indian population which
lacked immunity to European diseases in general is not surprising. The
Pouteotamis nation, one of the bravest and most loyal to the French,
almost perished to the point of extinction from this epidemic.[5] This was
indeed an unfortunate consequence, but it was not an act of Divine intervention.

Almost immediately after the carnage had ceased, the upper country Indians began carrying off their prisoners, hacking through the cemetery along the way in search of whatever morbid loot could be found. By
the next day most had made their departure up the lake en route to
Montreal. Meanwhile, Montcalm had sent a dispatch to Colonel Webb,
describing his plan of escorting the remaining survivors of the massacre
half way to Fort Edward, where they were to be met by a detatchment of
Regulars and escorted the remainder of the way to the English Fort.

The march commenced on August 15, when a very weary column
of nearly five hundred prisoners began stumbling through the gruesome
remains of the atrocity they had witnessed days eariler. Later that evening
the limp body of bandadged survivors arrived at Fort Edward. Others who
had managed to escape into the woods during the massacre had already
begun wandering in to the fort, some half naked, and others sick from
exposure. A cannon was fired every two hours as a directional aid to those
who had become disoriented during the fretful nightmare.

"About Noon ye Main Body of our People Came in from ye Lake
with their Coulers Displayd......all this Day our People Kept Coming in By
Small Partys Appearing in ye Most Pityfull Manner Som of them Stript
Intirely Naked other Robd of Most that they Had But Very few of them with
their Fire Locks. This & Yesterday are ye Two Most Sorrowful Days that
Ever were Known to N England.

I went with ye Working Party over to ye Island♣ to Make Fasheans

---

♣Rogers Island in Fort Edward

&c. This Day there was a Gun fired once in Two Hours to Call in our People that Had Got Lost in ye woods By Fleaing from ye Enimy which Signal Cald in Many of our Men....In ye Evening Col. Fry & Capt. Hitchcok Came in."[6]

As the main body of prisoners began their dismal departure from Lake George, a large detachment of English Regulars and Grenadiers were dispatched from Fort Edward to meet them at the half way point. This group of fortuitous survivors arrived at their destination during the evening hours of August 15th.

"In ye Morning all ye Grenodears with a Considrable Detatchment of ye Regulars was Sent of to Meet our prisoners who are at ye Lake.....ye Fore Part of ye Day was Rainy But it Cleared of about Noon.... Before Night our Party Returned with our People from ye Lake. Col. Monro Rid in on a Hors. Col. Young was brought in on a Bear. they Brought in a Small Brass Cannon with them..."[7]

The next few days at Fort Edward were spent providing medical aid, food, clothing and other necessities to the survivors of the massacre. Meanwhile, after all military stores had been despoiled, Montcalm prepared a written inventory which was then dispatched to Governor Vaudreuil. The following is the official register of the military stores supposedly sent by Montcalm to Carillon:

17 Pieces of Cannon, from 32 to five pounds, of which two brass and three iron are unfit for service.

  2 *9-inch mortars, burst during the seige*
  1 *9-inch Howitzer*
  1 *6-inch iron Mortar*
  13 *Small iron Swivels*
  1 *Shot Grating*
 227 *Barrels of powder of 100 lbs.*
 226 *Barrels of powder of 50 lbs.*
2,308 *Shot of diverse calibre*
 360 *6 & 9-inch Shell*
 185 *12 inch Shell*
  4 *Cases of Balls of 200 lbs.*
  1 *Case of Grenades*

> 6 Cases of Fireworks
> 6 Brass Guns, viz, 2 of 12, and 4 of 5 lbs.
> 4 Iron Swivels
> 215 Shot
> 75 Barrels of Powder of 25 lbs.
> 80 Gun Charges in caissons
> 600 Lbs. of Ball
> 50 Lbs. of Match
> 23 Cannon, of which 8 are brass
> 1 Fire Howitzer
> 1 Mortar
> 17 Swivels
> 35,835 Lbs. of Powder
> 2,522 Shot
> 1,400 Lbs. of Ball
> 1 Grenade Chest
> 6 Chests of Fireworks
>   Grapeshot of diverse Calibre
> 3,000 Barrels of flour or pork
>   All this property has been conveyed to Carillon.

Not surprisingly, this report bears no likeness to Monro's report, nor to the report sent from Carillon to Governor Vaudreuil at Montreal. The quantities listed hardly reflect an image of a fort supposedly suffering from lack of provisions.

At this time Montcalm's troops were engaged in dismantling what remained of Fort William Henry, and the agglomeration of scattered timbers was burned in a fire that lasted for two days. The intensity of the fire at Fort William Henry burnished the evening sky, a grim beacon of death seen sixteen miles away at Fort Edward.♣

"....also this Night ye French Burnt Fort Wm Henry....We Se ye

---

♣ Some accounts describe the French Troops gathering up the corpses of the dead and placing them upon the ruins of the fort before the blaze as a huge funeral pyre for the victims. There is no archaeological proof of this. Excavations along the South, East, and West Barracks between 1996 and 2000 have failed to produce even the slightest fragment of charred human bone. These findings are in agreement with those from the early Gifford excavations of the 1950's.

Light of ye Fire Most of ye Night. '**8** On August 21, Major Isreal Putnam was dispatched with a scouting party from Fort Edward to make a physical inspection of the damages sustained at Fort William Henry and report on the position and activity of the French army in the surrounding area, particularly along the military road. The following is a copy of Putnam's disconsolate report.

"The Fort was entirely destroyed; the barracks, outhouses, and buildings were a heap of ruins - the cannon, stores, boats, and vessels were all carried away. The fires were still burning; the smoke and stench offensive and suffocating. Innumerable fragments of human skulls, bones, and carcasses half-consumed, were still frying and broiling in the roasting fires. Dead bodies mangled with scalping knives and tomahawks, in all the wantonness of Indian barbarity, were everywhere to be seen. More than one hundred women butchered and shockingly mangled, lay upon the ground still weltering in their gore. Devastation, barbarity, and horror everywhere appeared; and the spectacle presented was too diabolical and awful either to be endured or described."

In late October, the last of the turnips still growing in the fort gardens were harvested by some Frenchmen who had sailed down the lake, a melancholy task rendered unappetizing by the occasional stench of decaying human flesh carried in the shifting gusts of the late autumn breeze. One month later, the ruins of Fort William Henry and its blood soaked surroundings would lie peacefully beneath a white shroud of winter snow.

---

[1]Documents Relative To The Colonial History Of The State Of New York Volume X Pg. 627 - 634 M. de Vaudreuil to M.de Moras

[2]Documents Relative To The Colonial History Of The State Of New York Volume X Pg. 627 - 634 M. de Vaudreuil to M.de Moras

[3]Documents Relative To The Colonial History Of The State Of New York Volume X Pg. 605 - 618 Bougainville to M. de Paulmy

[4]A History of the Town of Queensbury Pg. 6 Ref. Pouchot's Memoirs, Vol. 1, Pg.89

[5]The Diary of Jabez Fitch

[6] Carver's Travels

[7]The Diary of Jabez Fitch

[8]The Diary of Jabez Fitch

Chapter 10

The War Moves North

Ⅰf the year 1758 were to be recognized as a year of great accomplishments, it most certainly would not be recalled as the Year of the English
General. During July of that year, James Abercrombie, an ungainly
character of somewhat limited capacity, assembled an army of sixteen
thousand men at the head of Lake George to attack Fort Ticonderoga,
which at this time was manned by a garrison of approximately thirty two
hundred men under the Marquis de Montcalm. Bearing an acute similari-
ty to Braddock's expedition two years earlier, Abercombie's army
embarked from the southern end of the lake in 900 batteaux and well over
a hundred flatboats and whaleboats, forming a line nearly five miles long.
The mighty flotilla advanced proudly up the lake, its presence marked
by the insipid drone of bugle and bagpipe.

The French lines as they appear today at Ticonderoga

Montcalm's artillery entrenchments at the site of Abercrombie's defeat

The falls at the northern end of Lake George. This general area is the approximate location of the French sawmill in 1757.

Realizing that his army was substantially outnumbered and that provisions were low, Montcalm at Fort Ticonderoga ordered his men to build a jagged earthwork some distance from the fort in preparation for the English attack, sensing that the dim witted General would pursue the most direct line of approach. In front of the earthwork Montcalm's men created a morass of felled trees and sharpened stakes with the intention of obstructing the advance of the English army.

On July 6, Abercrombie's army landed at the north end of the lake and began falling into formation for the march against Ticonderoga. Just as Montcalm had expected, Abercrombie's men marched directly into the forest, tripping and stumbling over stumps and branches, and becoming entangled in the thick surrounding brush which the French had cut specifically for that purpose. Nearly 2,000 of Abercrombie's men were cut down by French musket fire during this engagement, marking one of the bloodiest battles of the French and Indian War. Those who were driven back were forced to take refuge in the several hundred outbuildings which Abercrombie had erected aaround the southern end of the lake prior to the attack, most of which were being used as hospitals for those retreating soldiers who had become sick or wounded. The expedition accomplished nothing other than to disgrace the brass of the English military, and complicate archaeological interpretations of the Fort William Henry site two

89

centuries later.

On June 21, 1759, Major General Jeffrey Amherst arrived at Lake George with an army of 11,000 men to once again attempt the capture of Fort Ticonderoga. *"This commander resolved, at all hazard, to retrieve the disaster of Abercrombie. He accordingly made every preparation to drive the French from Ticonderoga, and recover free use of the lakes."*[1] Amherst's rigid discipline was manifest from the very beginning of the campaign, causing many desertions. If not for the perpetual presence of Indians throughout the surrounding woods, these desertions would have been more frequent. Samuel Warner, a volunteer from Wilbraham, Massachusetts, describes the rather unrewarding march from Fort Edward to Lake George in his journal. *" Thursday 21 st this Day we marcht from fort Edward with about ten Regiments we struck our tents about brake of Day slong our packs aboout Sun Rise and stood ym (them) on a full ouer (hour) then marcht forward Nor onloaded Nor Rested till we got within five miles of Lake gorge there rested about one ouer and half varey hot men all- most Beet out By going without vittuals in the morning about 500 teems and waggins the officers had no packs the general and other big officers had horses and Servens they did not consider the poore Soldiers Had they Had any Compashoon (compssion) upon poore Soldiers they would not a dun as they Did one man Dyed by reason of such Hard travelling and Drinking of Warter this was a Connecticut man and two or three more it was said they ware a Dying the Army was marcht off in the morning on a sudden and had not time to git any Refreshment to Carey with them But God in His provi- dence has spared men's Lives & Carried them hather to we shall not Dey Before our time."*[2]

When Amherst arrived with his army at the southern end of the lake, he immediately ordered the chief engineer to draw plans for a new fortification east of the site of old Fort William Henry. *"In the evening he encamped on the banks of Lake George, and the next day, with the assis- tance of Colonel Montressor, the chief engineer, traced out the ground for the erection of a fort."*[3] The fort was laid out on a rocky prominence about 600 yards from the shore of the lake.

In an entry to his journal, another Massachusetts provincial depicts the site as "Element Hill," perhaps in reference to the abundance of lime- stone and clay available in the immediate vicinity, both raw materials being primary elements in the construction of the fort. *"The troops are employed in constructing a stone fortress fit to contain a garrison of six hundred men; it is of an irregular form, situated on a rock, has one front to the lake, and a large tract of morass surrounds the other faces of it; a casement is to be built in the fort, spacious enough to receive four hundred men at least; and there is plenty of good limestone, and excellent brick and clay on the spot."* ♣

On July 21, Amherst's army embarked on its mission to attack Fort Ticonderoga even though the work on Fort George had not been completed. The whaleboats and batteaux moved quietly up the lake, minus the grandeur of the Abercrombie fiasco a year earlier. Having faced opposition only from high winds, the army was put ashore in a small harbor at the northern end of the lake and began hauling the heavy artillery over the portage toward Ticonderoga. A very calculated two day bombardment of the fortress ensued, forcing the French army to evacuate the place and retreat north on Lake Champlain. On July 27, the Fort Ticonderoga was captured by the English and Provincial army, just as the southwest bastion of Fort George was completed.

The southern end of Lake George was of little strategic military significance following the fall of French power in North America. Fort George itself was never completed for this reason, and the ruins of the single completed bastion can be seen today in Fort George State Park. From the end of the Colonial wars to the beginning of the Revolution, Fort George was basically used as a transfer station and communications depot. The Governor issued a proclaimation announcing that the few inhabitants who had previously established their abodes in the vicinity of the fort could safely return to their homes.[4] This decree was premature, however, since the area did not again become safe for peaceful habitation until after the Revolutionary War.

General Burgoyne made use of the site during the Revolution, but after the war, decaying military structures like Fort George were abandoned, and the once battle scarred landscape at the southern end of Lake

---

♣ This entry was made in a journal by a person known only as Knox. The reference is probably to a provincial named John Knox, because Henry Knox was only 9 years of age at the time of the writing.

George now flourished with a number of small farms. Several Revolutionary War pensioners were granted patents for various tracts of land along the shores of the lake in an effort to attract settlers back to the region. One of these patents was granted to an Albany merchant named James Caldwell. Still known as the town of Caldwell in county records, this tract occupies the present day village of Lake George.

A time of peace was on the horizon. The terrifying thunder of cannon and musket which once echoed through the valley of death was no longer heard, and the screams of the dying had faded into the endless mist of time.

---

[1]The History of Fort George Pg. 4
[2]Willbraham Centennial Pg. 210
[3]History of the War in America Pg. 207
[4]The History of Fort George Pg. 8

Chapter 11

100 Years Later

One hundred years had now passed since the British flag was first raised at Fort William Henry. The icon of British military presence in North America which once served as the hub of military operations on Lake George, had now faded into the pages of history and folklore. The little hamlet bordering the southwest corner of the lake was known as Caldwell, named after James Caldwell, an Albany merchant who had been granted a patent for the scenic parcel in 1787. The year was now 1855, and public attention focused on the recently completed Fort William Henry Hotel built on a site just west of the old fort ruins.

Tourism was beginning to flourish in the Lake George region, the latter being made more accessible by growing improvements in mass transportation. The railroad reached as far as Glens Falls, where Lake George travelers would be met by a horse and carriage from the Glens Falls and Lake George Stage Company, which advertised new coaches, fast horses,

Guests at the Fort William Henry Hotel gathered for this early photograph

and historic scenery from the "Old French War." A wooden plank road had been built over the top of the miserably rutted old military road, significantly improving the comfort of the ride from Glens Falls to Lake George. The stage coach timetable was sensitive to the arrival and departure of both railroad and steamboat, accommodating the growing number of affluent visitors not only to the Fort William Henry Hotel, but to a number of other hotels and inns which had established themselves in the surrounding Lake George area. A regional attraction pamphlet published in 1884 describes even the short trip between the railroad station in Lake George to the Fort William Henry Hotel as interesting.

"The space traversed in going to and from the cars is rich in history and tradition and was once the centre of vast military operations, which brought together a host four times greater than could now find quarters in all the hotels and cottages along Lake George's teeming shores; now we go through winding paths, under stately pines that grow on the ramparts and in the trenches, where men of old watched for the savage foe or made merry around the barrack fire. Situated, as the hotel is, at the very head of the lake, it catches its share of the faintest breath that blows, its open position affording the winds from the south through the valley, and those from the north over the far reaching water, full sweep and it is seldom that there is not enough moving to stir its surface.

Of great interest to the antiquarian will be found the cabinet of ancient curiosities; relics gathered through many years from the fort and battlefield, from the forest, and even the bottom of the lake, rude implements of aboriginal home-life and savage warfare, side by side with the more modern arm of French and English, who here contended nearly a century and a quarter ago, each with its unwritten history, and its suggestions of the dead past."[1]

The Fort William Henry Hotel was extravagant, having 450 rooms and a carriage house capable of boarding private horses and carriages. It boasted of suites, hot baths, and live music. High speed telecommunication services were also available in the form of the telegraph, which connected with all lines throughout the state and gave a full stock market report three times daily!

After a few hard sets of tennis played on a court built near the old military cemetery, a visitor could relax with a bottle of ginger beer on the porch of the hotel, or in a gazebo near the ruins of the old fort, a densely overgrown mound of earth now laced with a number of walking paths for the benefit of those wishing to get a first hand glimpse of history. Following an evening meal in the hotel dining room, a visitor could put his dexterity to the test at "Ten Pin Alley," an outdoor bowling lane which had been built near the spot where the northeast bastion of the fort once stood. This was the advent of tourism in the area, a haven offering unparalleled scenery, historical significance, fine accommodations, and a diverse variety of activities.

Tourism continued to grow vigorously in the Lake George region, aided by the extension of the railroad from Glens Falls in 1882. Passengers arrived at the newly built railroad station where a number of steamboats offered a product of fine cuisine and breathtaking scenery while transporting visitors to a variety of destinations on the lake. Over land, the trolley eventually replaced what remained of the horse and carriage trade, and by the early 20th century, the largest impact on the region both economically and environmentally was made by the combustion engine.

The introduction of the automobile triggered a new mutation in travel patterns which unfortunately had a negative imact on the once popular large hotel. As early as 1905, motorists were stopping for the night at small groups of cottages known as tourist courts. These would later become known as motor courts, many of which continue to flourish in the area today. By the early 1950's, the typical elongated roadside structure known as the motel had been born, marking the beginning of a new trend in accommodations for travelling motorists.

On June 24, 1909, the Fort William Henry Hotel burned to the ground. The structure was rebuilt two years later, having less than half the capacity of the original. The hotel survived for approximately 50 years, at which time it was deemed structurally unsafe, and with the exception of the original elegant dining room and adjacent kitchen, the building was demolished, marking the end of an era. The 19th century phenomenon known as the *hotel de grand luxe* once popular in Europe had now also faded into the pages of American History.

---

[1]Lake George, A Book of Today   Stoddard

Chapter 12

First Archaeology: The Gifford Years

By the middle of the twentieth century, Lake George had evolved into a popular vacation spot. The quiet village of Caldwell now flourished with souvenier shops, hot dog stands and ice cream parlors. With each passing year, vacant properties were being swiftly gobbled up by those wishing to capitalize on the growing number tourists coming to the area.

It is almost uncanny that the ruins of the old fort remained untouched for such an extended period of time. As early as 1882 there was a dismal plan on the table to level the historic site in order to accommodate a number of additional railroad storage buildings. Harold Veeder and Alden Shaw were two area businessmen who recognized this ever growing threat to the old Fort William Henry property and decided to purchase the historic parcel themselves. The Fort William Henry Corporation was formed and Stanley Gifford, an archaeologist from the western part of the

97

Looking north along the east side of the fort circa 1950.

state was hired to head up the archaeology team. Photostatic copies of original maps, drawings, and other manuscripts relating to Fort William Henry were procured from both the British and Canadian Archives, the Library of Congress, and the New York State Museum. These documents were studied for many hours before a systematic approach to the excavation was drawn up.

The first step was to remove the dense overgrowth of trees from the site, a task made easier through the use of heavy equipment supplied by the town, and through volunteer laborers. Even as the first stumps were yanked from the ground, artifacts lying just inches beneath the surface began to appear. Laborers were asked to set these items aside for later examination, since the limited size of the archaeology team made it impossible to supervise all of the excavation areas simultaneously. Due to this unfortunate circumstance, a countless number of musket balls, bayonets, cannon balls and other artifacts disappeared into the backs of pickup trucks and taken out of their historic context, surely to be seen by some future generation as nothing but old junk.

Once the overgrowth had been removed from the site, the serious task of locating and identifying features from the original fort was begun. Four mounds of earth were all that remained of fort's original four bastions. The slight depression separating them had once been the parade ground.

Early guided tour of the archaeological sites

Seal is removed from unexploded mortar bomb.

An inverted wooden box served as cover for the old fort well. Since the northwest bastion of the fort suffered most severely from the French bombardment, it is not surprising that a large number of artifacts were discovered in this area. Ten kegs of various calibre musket balls were unearthed, one mortar which had been split from overuse, and a preponderance of mortar

99

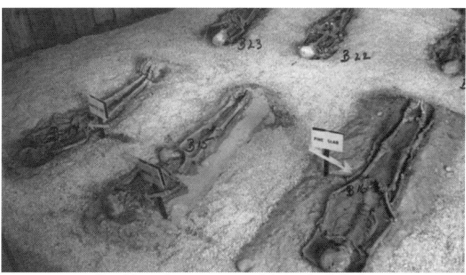

Six of the twelve graves exposed during the Gifford era.

bomb fragments. A small powder magazine was also discovered here. The main magazine was discovered under the northeast bastion, along with a portion of the brick lined passage leading to the underground structure. The outline of twelve grave shafts had been marked in the military cemetery, and incomplete human skeletal remains were being discovered on other areas of the property. One mass grave containing five skeletons was discovered along the east side of the parade ground of the fort.

In some of the deeper pits, a significant prehistoric component was beginning to turn up in the artifact mix. A temporary museum building was erected to display the unique archaeological discoveries to the general public, who at this time were led by a tour guide over a predetermined path woven between the dig sites.

One of the more unusual discoveries was that of an unexploded mortar bomb, the only discovery of its kind on the continent. Even more unusual was the fact that this particular bomb had human hair embedded in the resin seal. Bomb specialists were called upon to disarm the device, and the separated resin seal now gave the appearance of a scalp. After being further analyzed in a lab, the hair was determined to be human, black, and very old.

Even though the archaeological findings at Fort William Henry were becoming ever more interesting, the financial picture at the newly

100

Tour guide Jack McEneny demonstrates proper handling of an 18th century musket.

formed corporation was somewhat less inspiring. With little revenue to balance out two years of cash outlays for research and other expenses, the Fort William Henry Corporation was now faced with financial disaster. At this time Albany businessman and local motel owner Edwin "Babe" McEnaney, was approached for possible assistance to help save the financially compromised project. It will never be fully known why Mr. McEnaney was willing to take the risk, but through the memory of the author's mother, he is recalled as being *"concerned over the Coney Island image that Lake George was taking on."* Hence the corporation was restructured so that shares of preferred stock became common stock, and through both family and business associates, Mr. McEnaney was able to raise enough capital to pay off creditors and complete the reconstruction. If not for Mr. McEnaney's financial wisdom, the Fort William Henry project would have fallen just as quickly as its 18th century predecessor.

Stanley Gifford was the first curator at the fort, and work was begun immediately doing research and preparing exhibits for the main museum. The tour guides now dressed in 18th century attire and performed military demonstrations such as musket and cannon firings. Archaeological pits were filled in, and from that point forward thousands of visitors would pass through the gate of Fort William Henry to re-live the story made so famous by James Fenimore Cooper.

101

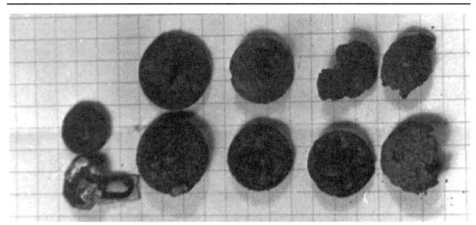

Cuff Links and buttons found at the Birch Avenue grave site.

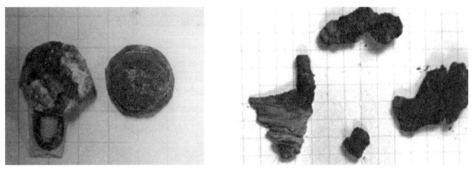

Cuff link with wood and oxidized nail fragments found at the Birch Avenue site

Over the next several years as new motels, homes, restaurants and roads were being constructed in the area surrounding Lake George, the ground upon which these structures were laid out continued to yield grim clues of a brutal past. This was apparent as early as the mid-19th century. "While digging cellars for his house (1860) and vault for ice-house (1867), Dr. James Crommel of Lake George exhumed thirteen skulls." [1]

Similar discoveries were still commonplace during the construction boom that occurred during the mid-twentieth century. Perhaps the most significant of these discoveries was made on March 24, 1965 by a local construction crew while digging the foundation of a motel and swimming pool near Birch Avenue in Lake George. Twenty eight graves were unearthed during the initial stages of construction.

The greatest number of graves uncovered showed little indication whatsoever that the bodies had been interred in coffins; however, a cross-section of one grave showed the definite outline of a coffin, and fragments of oxidized iron and a nail embedded in wood were recovered from this grave.

" Sept. 25, 1755   This morning I got a coffin made for Capt. Hawley and at 11 of ye clock fore noon attended his funeral ... ye funeral was attended with decency and order.'[2]   Capt. Hawley had received a wound in action Sept.8th, from which he died on Sept. 14th, 1755.

One skeleton in this mass grave was very significant, showing signs of mutilation, with both the head and a number of cervical vertebra missing. The arms had been carefully laid across the front of the body at the time of burial. This particular grave was excavated by hand from ground level to the bottom of the grave. The individual who performed the actual digging is unknown; however, a brief written record was kept and photographs were taken of the activity by the late James A. Magee, who at that time was the curator at Fort William Henry. The following were his observations:

"The head was completely missing from this skeleton. It was excavated entirely by hand and there was no indication that the grave had ever been disturbed prior to this excavation. Fine tree rootlets had grown into the neck vertabrae as shown in the photograph. Underneath this skeleton were found the metal cuff link, one of the uniform buttons, the fragment

Decapitated skeleton from the Birch Avenue site.

of a great coat with the button hole intact, this having been preserved by the metallic salts from the button. A fragment of fine linen shirt cuff was also preserved from the salts of the cuff link. A large gun flint was also found on the skeleton's right side located approximately under the pocket position of the great coat. The writer of these notes excavated this grave personally and can vouch for the accuracy of the above statement."

44 ft. sloop seen by historian Francis Parkman in 1842 and brought ashore by amateur divers in 1903. Note the railroad tracks extending on to the steamboat dock.

The property owner, eager to proceed with the construction, allowed only four days to gather information about the graveyard. The bones were then removed and re-buried at an undisclosed location. We may never know if Capt. Hawley was buried there, but the location of the plot, the artifact mix, and historical reference suggests this may have been the burying place for those who died during the Battle of Lake George in 1755. If this is true, there are over 100 more burials somewhere in the surrounding area.

The lake itself was also yielding clues of its wartime past. As early as 1903, amateur divers had pulled up the charred remains of a 44 ft. sloop on to the shore adjacent to the steamboat dock. This is believed to have been one of the sloops burned by Vaudreiul's army during the winter of 1757. When historian Francis Parkman visited the Lake George region in 1842, he apparently saw this vessel submerged near the southern shore of the lake. In Volume I of his journals Parkman writes, *"The spikes and timbers of sunken vessels may be seen in strong sunlight, when the water is still, at the bottom of the lake, along the southern beach. '*[3]

After its discovery in 1903, the vessel remained on the shoreline for only a short time before its decaying framework was broken apart and the pieces taken as souveniers. One large section is preserved at Fort William Henry. Other items such as anchors, rum bottles, mortar bombs, and muskets were discovered in the lake as docks and boathouses were being built. In many cases these artifacts were brought to the fort for identification, and

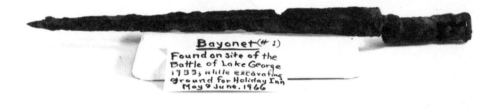

Bayonet discovered during the construction of the Lake George Holiday Inn.

some were put on exhibit. These discoveries in the surrounding area painted a very broad,
vivid picture of both Fort William Henry and 18th century Lake George.

During the summer season, the report of the cannon was heard every hour, as thousands of fascinated visitors witnessed military demonstrations given by uniformed tour guides. The tradition carried on over the next several years until autumn of 1967 when an arson fire destroyed the entire west barracks building of the fort, the southwest bastion, the museum, and the gift shop. Many artifacts were recovered, but many were lost, making the episode akin to the many chronicles of misfortune with which the fort seemed to be cursed. Due to the diligence of corporation president Robert Flacke Sr., reconstruction was begun immediately. By the following season, the fort was restored to operational capacity, but the preponderance of catalogue work needed to be done made even the most astute auditor think of searching for a new line of employment.

Two early photographs of the Fort William Henry parade ground.

Two grim photographs showing the damage caused by the fire of 1967.

Fire damage inside the west barracks building.

[1]Chronicles of Lake George   *Journeys in War and Peace*   Pg. 289

[2]The Journals and Papers of Seth Pomeroy   Pg. 119

[3]The Journals of Francis Parkman   Volume I   Pg. 48

Chapter 13

The Influence of Hollywood

Tourists continued to visit Fort William Henry each season and the boom of the cannon was again heard echoing through the mountains. The guided tours resumed their normal schedule, but after Mr. Gifford's passing in the 1960's, further archaeological exploration at the fort was not undertaken. By 1992, it was not archaeology, but Hollywood which sparked interest in the old fort with Michael J. Mann's production of *"Last of the Mohicans."*

Soon after the development of the motion picture in 1890, Hollywood began making film versions of literary classics such as Victor Hugo's *"Hunchback of Notre Dame,"* and biblical epics like *"The Ten Commandments."* It was only a matter of time before the Cooper classic, *"Last of the Mohicans,"* was swept from the pages of American literature into the Hollywood Studio. Several twisted versions of the film were produced over the years, each offering its own distortion of the original work. Hollywood made four silent film versions of the film between 1920 and 1931. Harry Carey starred in a twelve chapter serial in 1932. The longest

109

1936 marquis for the movie, "Last of the Mohicans"

lasting version starring Randolph Scott was filmed in 1936. Other, inferi-
or versions followed in 1947, 1952, 1965, 1977, and 1979. Cartoon versions of the film were also made in the United States, Germany, and
Australia.

Then on September 25, 1992, Hollywood film maker Michael
Mann's *"Last of the Mohicans,"* starring Daniel Day-Lewis, was shown in
theaters for the first time. This release has proven without a doubt to be the
most popular film version of the story ever produced.   The film contains
some minor historical inaccuracies, but these are offset by a multiple of
authenticities, specifically the film's more realistic depiction of collisions
between European and Native American cultures.

Even the hand made wigs worn by actors portraying British soldiers in the film are accurate down to the most minute detail, at an expense
of $1,500. per piece. In comparison to previous versions there is consid-
erable violence in the movie, and although various sequences contain some
degree of imagination, the violence itself was not something created by the
producers of the film. The warfare methods portrayed in the movie were

commonly practiced by a number of ethnohistorical groups during the 18th century.

Stars of the film include Daniel Day-Lewis, and stunningly beautiful co-star, Madeliene Stowe. Mann hired Native Americans, including Activist Russell Means, founder of the American Indian Movement (AIM), to play the roles of Indians, despite the fact that Means had no prior acting experience. Aside from getting a crash course in acting, Means had to be trained in old Indian skills. Both He and Daniel Day-Lewis, cast as Chingachgook and Hawkeye, trained for weeks at a survival camp in Alabama where they learned to literally live off the wilderness. Also attending the camp was Wes Studi, a Cherokee Indian who played the eerily venomous Magua, renegade Huron warrior. Studi's characterization of the Native American is an accurate portrayal of an 18th century Sachem. The stereotypical "what-him-say" dialect so often associated with amiss Hollywood portrayals of the Native American was categorically obliterated by Studi's performance. In addition to his ferocity, Magua is seen as both intelligent and emotional, yet capable of the same treachery used by both the French and the English.

Because of the commercial atmosphere surrounding Fort William Henry in Lake George, an alternative site was chosen for the filming of the movie. While the actors were engaged in wilderness training, a full scale replica of the fort was built on beautiful Lake James, a little known lake seated in the middle of the Blue Ridge mountains in North Carolina. This wilderness setting was not unlike that which surrounded the southern extremity of Lake George two hundred and fifty years ago. Construction of the mock fortress took three months to complete at an estimated cost of six million dollars. This was the largest set ever to be constructed east of the Mississippi.

In addition to the fort, a twenty acre farmstead, a Huron village, and the Colonial Village of Albany were all constructed in North Carolina. After the completion of the movie, the entire set including the fort, the farmstead, the Indian village, and the village of Albany were dismantled and hauled away. The site was leveled and the trees replanted. Today on Lake James, no trace of Hollywood's brief presence in the area is discernable to the eye. The final budget for the blockbuster film was estimated at forty million dollars.

In 1993, Fort William Henry became the highlight of the television camera as the Discovery Channel, in collaboration with several local scientists, ran a series which would provide new scientific angles on old interpretations.

111

A Proper Burial

Pristine skies and a tranquil breeze marked the beginning of this day, as Mother Nature seemed to cast her seal of approval over the solemn ceremony which was about to get under way. The remains of soldiers uncovered during archaeological work at Fort William Henry had now been returned to the ground, and a small group of invited guests had gathered at this spot for the "Memorial Cemetery Dedication," in solemn commemoration not only of these soldiers, but all of the unfortunate men and women who had lost their lives in this almost forgotten war. In attendance were Chief Paul Waterman of the Onondaga Nation; Senator Ronald B. Stafford; Rep. James King; Dr. David Starbuck; Tim Gurney, Deputy Director of British Information Services; Lt. Col. John Silvester, H.M. 49th, 62nd, 66th, and 99th Regiments; and the late Rev. Jack Williams of St. James Episcopal Church in Lake George.

Corporation president Robert Flacke Sr. opened the proceedings with an introductory speech, followed by the most poignant moment of the entire program. A very frail Chief Waterman was assisted to the podium where he addressed the somber congregation in his native tongue, interpretation being provided by his daughter. Following a brief speech by Lt. Col Silvester, an invocation was offered by Rev. Williams, and a great floral wreath was placed over a granite monument by both Lt. Col. Silvester and Chief Waterman. The monument reads:

"This Marker Commemorates those Men and Women who Died in the Siege Of Fort William Henry 1n 1757.
Exhumed during Archaeological Excavations in 1953, their Remains were given This Final Resting Place on May 30, 1993"

The formalities concluded after Chief Waterman's group buried a small quantity of co rn bread, an ancient symbolic ritual of providing nourishment for the deceased on their journey to the afterlife. In one hour of American History in which cultural differences were of no distinction, two hundred and thirty six years of dignity to a dark shadow of American History had been restored.

Chapter 14

The Massacre under the Microscope

D ue to the absence of sophisticated laboratory equipment in the 1950's, most of Gifford's historical interpretations relied heavily on visual observation. This was especially true with respect to the human remains discovered, not only in the cemetery, but on other parts of the property. When a small portion of burial ground was discovered adjacent to the present day parking area, a log building was built over the plot to protect the twelve exposed grave shafts from the elements. After the skeletons were completely exposed, several distinct observations were made. One skeleton had a lead musket ball embedded in the left elbow, while the remains of a bandage and bandage pin were still wrapped around the neck of another. These examples suggest possible causes of death. Other observations suggest this may have been an officer's burial plot.

112

Mass grave discovered in the parade ground of the fort.

One skeleton had been carefully laid out on a coffin-like pine slab prior to burial, and cufflinks were discovered on another. All interpretations were limited to the realm of hypothesis, and in the absence of high level scientific capability, no further research was ever done on these skeletons. They were treated with a preservative and left on display as an archaeological exhibit for nearly forty years.

Other skeletons, both complete and incomplete, were found on the property, one of which was discovered accidentally by a construction worker who was laying a water line. This skeleton was found in a hunched over position under the southwest bastion. Still others exhibited skull fractures apparently caused by tomahawk blows. A mass grave containing the skeletal remains of five men was also discovered on the east side of the parade ground. These men had been hastily buried in one of the cellar areas of the buildings along the east curtain. One of these skeletons showed evidence of amputation, while yet another was missing a skull. It seems more than coincidental that this was the very spot where Father Robaud had witnessed the decapitation of an Englishman two hundred years earlier. The speculation and skepticism surrounding this issue and others would not begin to abate until advances in technology and forensic pathology provided new avenues of interpretation.

In December of 1993, Archaeology Magazine ran a feature story

113

Further exposure of the mass grave in the parade ground.

called *"Anatomy of a Massacre"* by David R. Starbuck. Dr. Starbuck, an expert in the field of colonial history, had excavated sites all around New England, including Mt. Defiance in Vermont and Rogers Island in Fort Edward, New York. *"Anatomy of a Massacre"* revisited the two year existence of Fort William Henry with the aid of archival photographs from the Gifford era. At this time it was apparent that the human remains which had been on exhibit for forty years were beginning to show advanced stages of deterioration. Questions concerning ethics and the social acceptability of such exhibits also lingered. After a careful review of these sensitive issues, final interment of the remains was prudently agreed upon. Dr. Starbuck providied his professional expertise and suggestions with respect to the matter.

At that time Dr. Maria Liston, Osteoarchaeologist at Adirondack Community College, and Dr. Brenda Baker from the State Museum in Albany, were given permission to study the skeletal remains at Fort William Henry prior to their final burial. The entire project was filmed and later telecast over the Learning channel in an episode aptly entitled , *"Last of the Mohicans."*

The results of Dr. Baker and Dr. Liston's research reveal that these soldiers suffered from a shocking variety of maladies. The unprovenienced bones (bones of incomplete skeletons not belonging to the same

114

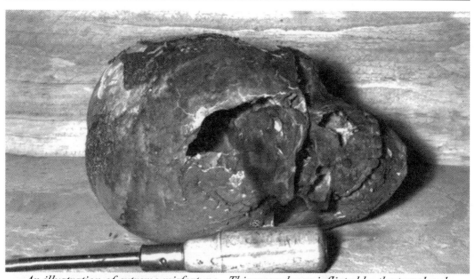

An illustration of extreme misfortune. This wound was inflicted by the tomahawk.

person), were discovered to have belonged to sixteen different individuals, the youngest of whom was approximately fourteen years of age. A significant number suffered from problems such as herniated disks and osteoarthritis, both conditions resulting from prolonged exposure to extreme physical stress. Ten of the sixteen skeletons exhibited cranial injuries, fractures, amputations, and other evidence of perimortem trauma. Two amputations were apparent, one of which had been terminated.

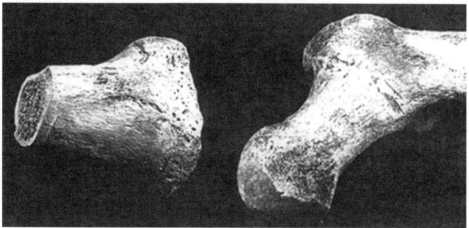

Left: Unhealed amputated right tibia.
Right: Partial amputation of proximal femur.

115

The saw marks on the femur of the left leg suggest that this individual died before the limb could be removed. In the second amputation, removal of the limb was successful; however, the amputation area shows no indication of healing, suggesting that death probably followed soon after.

One of the five skeletons discovered in the parade ground exhibited cranial damage inflicted by some type of heavy instrument with a point,

Cranial trauma and possible cause. Lower arrow points to probable scraping caused by the scalping knife. Note the large puncture and radiating fractures, possibly inflicted by a war club similar to the one shown in the right hand illustration..

possibly a war club. The sharp point pierced the skull, while the weight of the instrument caused smaller, radiating fractures. The adjacent scraping marks represent the morbid signature left by the scalping knife. Another skeleton was missing a skull. The second cervical vertebra of the odontoid process of this skeleton exhibits a pattern of four cut marks indicating that this poor unfortunate was beheaded. The pattern of the cuts also suggests that the decapitation was somewhat less than immediate. These findings lend credence to Father Robaud's sickening observations immediately after the surrender of the fort in 1757.

In many cases, the medical treatment of injuries sustained at Fort William Henry proved to be equally as fatal as the injuries themselves. Patients were given large draughts of Jamaican rum as a substitute for anesthesia, and during times of excruciating pain, the hapless soul marked for the operating table was given a lead musket ball on which to

116

clamp his teeth. Musket balls with teeth marks imbedded deeply in them have been found during excavations at the fort. Rib fractures on all of the skeletons suggest repeated blows to both the front and rear of the rib cage with an axe or tomahawk, possibly to gain access to the chest cavity. Mutilation was practiced by both Europeans and some Native American groups during the 18th century.

"About 8 oClok Gen. Lyman Came in from His Scout, they Brought in News that they found Henry Shuntup in ye woods Kild & Scalped His throat Cut & His Brest Cut open & Hart out...."[1]

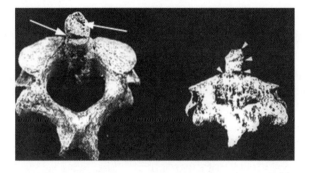

Cut marks on the axis vertabra of beheaded undividual.

In addition to physical wounds, the soldiers suffered from a myriad of other problems as well. Lesions on both the vertebrae and ribs indicate the presence of chronic respiratory infections such as pneumonia, chronic bronchitis, and tuberculosis. Similar lesions on the temporal bones of at least one skeleton suggest ear infection. A number of skeletons were missing teeth which apparently had become abscessed. This was a common affliction during the 18th century due mostly to lack of dental hygiene. A Connecticut Provincial named Jabez Fitch had apparently suffered at least once from the condition. *"...About noon I went over ye river into ye camp....then I came back and Doctor Adams Puld a Tooth for Me...."*[2]

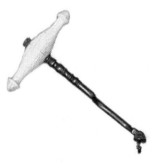

Eighteenth Century tooth extractor

Excessive porosity in the skull

bone of one skeleton suggests that this individual was anemic, a condition possibly brought on by iron deficiency, parasite load, or both. In their final manuscript dealing with the mass grave in the courtyard, Dr. Liston and Dr. Baker arrived at the following conclusion.

"The evidence gleaned from the analysis of the remains buried together inside the fort confirms and enhances the ethnohistorical and later fictionalized accounts of the massacre at Fort William Henry. Four of the five individuals in this mass grave had leg trauma, which would have significantly impeded their mobility as the garrison retreated to Fort Edward. The massive trauma and mutilation on all five skeletons surpasses even the most lurid accounts of the massacre. One individual was, indeed, beheaded. Three of the five men were shot in the knee; two of these men were shot elsewhere as well. All of the men sustained gashes on both the front and back of their bodies from multiple swings of an axe. One also appears to have been stabbed in the back with a knife. At least one man was apparently able to defend himself to a limited extent, suffering cut marks on his left wrist and a blow to the underside of his right foot.

The pattern of cuts and gashes strongly suggests that these men were mutilated possibly to obtain trophies. The head was taken from one man; scalps may have been taken from others, but the lack of extant cranial remains does not allow us to verify those reports in this context. In all the men, ribs were cut or fractured at the sternal ends or sides, probably to obtain access to the chest cavity so that the heart could be reached. The fact that the pubic area was cut in all of the men suggests genital mutilation. The extent of destruction in the abdominal and chest cavities indicates the men may also have been disemboweled. Thus, the accounts of the massacre at Fort William Henry were, if anything, understatements of the actual event." [3]

It was not easy to be alive at Fort William Henry in 1757 be you man, woman, or child. The name of the game was death, and brutality and disease were rolling the dice.

---

[1] The Diary of Jabez Fitch Jr.

[2] The Diary of Jabez Fitch Jr.

[3] Reconstructing the Massacre at Fort William Henry   Maria A. Liston,   Brenda J. Baker 1995

Chapter 15

1997: Reviving a Legend

In October 1995, Dr. Liston and Dr. Baker returned to Fort William Henry to do follow up work on the research done in 1993. Because the extent of Fort William Henry's military cemetery is unknown, one goal was to determine if intact graves still existed, given the more recent use of the site as a resort hotel and tourist attraction. The second goal was to evaluate the integrity and extent of prehistoric occupation, based on findings two years earlier. The first goal raised an interesting question, given the fact that a good portion of the cemetery had been violated over a decade before the first Fort William Henry Hotel was even constructed. When historian Francis Parkman visited the area in 1842, he made the following observations.

"The old fort is much larger than I had thought; the earthen mounds cover many acres. It stood on the southwest extremity of the lake close by the water. The enterprising genius of the inhabitants has made a road directly through the ruins, and turned bastion, moat, and glacis into

119

a flourishing cornfield, so that the spot so celebrated in our colonial his-
tory is now scarcely to be distinguished. Large trees are growing on the
untouched parts, especially on the embankment along the lake shore. In
the rear, a hundred or two yards distant, is a gloomy wood of pines, where
the lines of Montcalm can easily be traced. A little behind these lines is the
burying place of the French who fell during that memorable seige. * *The*
marks of a thousand graves can be seen among the trees, which, of course
have sprung up since. Most of them have been opened, and bones and
skulls dug up in great numbers." ♣

Despite ostensibly poor odds, the outcome of this project was pos-
itive. The following is an excerpt from the conclusion of Dr. Baker's final
report. "Both goals of the project were met. Eight graves dating to the
fort's occupation between 1755 and 1757 were located. Seven features,
including both prehistoric and historic hearths, and large quantities of artifacts were discovered. Prehistoric artifacts indicate both Archaic and
Woodland components, the latter supported by a radiocarbon date from a
hearth feature. Most historic artifacts date to the nineteenth century,
reflecting use of the area as a resort. Eighteenth century material includes
objects interred with the three excavated burials, and fragments of
stoneware, glass, and pipe stems. Analysis of the artifacts and features
found in a relatively small area reveals the importance of this site beyond
its notoriety as a military outpost during the French and Indian War." [1]

The popularity of both the *"Last of the Mohicans"* film and television broadcasts by the Discovery Channel depicting the subsequent
archaeological work done at the Fort William Henry site spurred a period
of robust curiosity at Fort William Henry. An increasing number of questions were being asked by visitors concerning the exact location of the original fort, the accuracy of the reconstruction, the extent of the original excavations, and so on.

At this particular time Dr. David Starbuck, Professor of
Archaeology at Plymouth State University in New Hampshire, had been
conducting an Archaeological field school offered through Adirondack

---

♣ Parkman's positioioning of the overall cemetery is accurate, however a bit misleading. The
French did not sustain one thousand casualties during the engagement at Fort William during the
summer of 1757. It is likely however, that French casualties were buried on their own side of the
Montcalm's artillery entrenchments.

Community College. In 1996, the group was involved in excavations on Rogers Island in Fort Edward, NY, the 18th century British stronghold seated at the most northern navigable point of the Hudson River. The island derives its name from Capt. Robert Rogers, the fabled New Hampshire provincial who founded the special forces group known as Rogers' Rangers.

It had been over fifty years since the original archaeological work was undertaken at Fort William Henry, and aside from the recent work done by Dr. Liston and Dr. Baker in the cemetery area, nothing of any significance was ever done in the Fort proper from an archaeological perspective. Following a series of meetings between Dr. Starbuck and fort officials, a proposed field school of six weeks duration at Fort William Henry was arranged for the summer of 1997, a project which would continue for three contiguous seasons. Research was begun immediately.

Due to the disastrous fire in 1967, any records kept by Stanley Gifford during the 1950's are assumed to have been destroyed. Indeed, artifacts discovered during those years had been identified and catalogued, but precise information on location, depth, or related specifics which might otherwise prove helpful remained elusive. As a result, Dr. Starbuck and a number of crew chiefs spent many hours scouring over old photographs, newspaper articles, architectural drawings (both original and contemporary), insurance maps,

Cross beam over the well

121

and many other sources in search of information which might prove helpful to the project. Even the most inconsequential clues were welcomed and examined.

Following a considerable period of research, the most probable dig sites were narrowed to four basic areas. The first was the fort well, a project which for safety reasons was abandoned during the 1960's. The second was a small plot at the northeast corner of the parade ground, which in reality was an extension of Gifford's trench along the east curtain during the 1950's. This area was chosen based on photographs of the old trench depicting its point of termination. A third site was opened outside the east curtain wall. One of the goals in this area was to intersect the military access road leading from the beach up to the original entrance to the fort which was located in the southeast bastion. The fourth site was adjacent to the parking area, near the place where a significant Native American component was discovered two years earlier.

Of the four sites chosen, the well was the most technically challenging. A ten foot high, strut mounted cross beam was built over the feature to support a chain hoist which was used to lower two sections of a three and one half foot diameter steel culvert into the two hundred and fifty year old vertical shaft as a precaution against cave-ins. An electric hoist was mounted on the beam to haul out the hundreds of buckets of sand which were then sifted for artifacts. Dr. Starbuck did the actual digging, the bottom of the stone cabal made accessible by a diminutive seat which was also raised and lowered by means of the electric hoist. Every minute of the digging activity was captured by an observation camera mounted inside the culvert, the video signal then suitably routed to a remote television monitor which provided visitors with a safe viewing perspective.

There were no fastidious expectations with respect to the excavation of the well. In the world of folklore, Col. Monro, in an epic moment of emotional perseverance, gallantly tossed the fort payroll into the well at the time of capitulation. In other such preposterous nightmares, small children were snatched from their mothers by Indians and thrown down the dreaded stone hollow, a dismal legend which has survived in the glamour of the campfire for over two centuries. From a practical perspective, anything capable of being tossed through the air at the time the fort was under seige might possibly have come to rest in the bottom of the well. With
122

these facts in mind, Dr. Starbuck's archaeology team prepared themselves to search for clues.

The early stages of digging progressed with few problems. The bottom of the well at this time was approximately twelve feet below the surface of the ground. Water had not yet become a major problem, so the task of removing gravel, coins, and other tourist deposits spanning several decades was begun, a miserable occupation which was accomplished one bucketful at a time. Every item best suited to be found elswhere on the face of the earth seemed to turn up in the bottom of the well. Sunglasses, golf tees, flash cubes, bulbs, chewing gum, cigarette lighters, golf balls, and diapers are just a few examples representing what can wholly be described as hopelessly inane human impulse. Thousands of coins from around the world were discovered, dating back to the turn of the century. Moving back a little further in time, an impeccable ginger beer bottle dating to the late 19th century was found, along with a round wooden object believed to be one of the balls used at "Ten Pin

Bowling ball from "Ten Pin Alley"

Alley," the aforementioned outdoor bowling lane known to exist near the spot in 1876. In a manner of wit, your author later characterized the spherical breakthrough as "the ultimate gutter ball."

After fourteen linear feet of these modern day residuals had been removed from the well, water slowly began appearing. Digging continued until the water reached a depth of approximately six inches. At this time digging was halted while a high volume pump was configured for the difficult
task of keeping the well free of water for the duration of the excavation.

The cross beam over the well was now an impressive complexity of swtches, cables, and wires. A drainage hose resembling a large, black serpent lay curled near the opening. Each day Dr. Starbuck was lowered into the well, troweling the heavy silt into buckets, while your author operated the hoist and ensured the general safety of the project from the surface. After being hoisted to the top, each bucket was sifted for artifacts, and the bucket was once again lowered to the bottom of the momentous shaft. This "production line" process was employed for the duration of the project. Literally thousands of gallons of water were pumped from the well each day, as the performance capacity of the pump scarcely outpaced the well's recovery rate. The project was halted a number of times due to unexpected power failures and miserable lightning storms. These situations necessitated Dr. Starbuck's immediate departure from the steel lined cylinder, a sodden but familiar excursion during which the inadequacy of rubber boots was most thoroughly demonstrated.

Foregoing the discovery of 18th century artifacts in the well, a large quantity of organic material was found in the form of pine cones, branches, and skeletal remains of various rodents and small animals, including those of a goose. A closer examination of the goose carcass revealed that the right ulna (wingbone), had broken and then healed in a

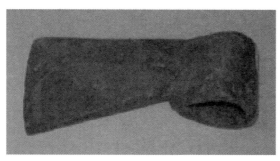

deformed manner, indicating that this particular goose was unable to fly when it arrived at its unfortunate destination. It has been well documented that soldiers kept a variety of wild animals as pets during the eighteenth century. Whether or not the goose was deliberately thrown into the well to prevent further use of it

Trade Axe found beneath the east barracks

cannot be said with any degree of certainty, but the scenario is unlikely because the well during that time was already filthy, hardly in need of further contamination.

The mix of eighteenth century artifacts discovered in the well included musket balls, window glass, pottery sherds, and several French gun flints. The most unique discovery, however, was in the very construction of the well itself. The bottom portion of the well was found to be constructed of wood. This wooden cylinder consisted of three inch thick

124

planks ranging in width from seven to twelve inches, carefully fitted together in a shape closely resembling the hot tub of today. There were a number of carefully bored holes, behind which lay a deposit of finer stones. Three feet of this 18th century filtration system was eventually exposed, and the overall length of the boards measured at least five feet. At this time the discharge line was becomming jammed with silt, as the force of incomming water began to overwhelm our pumping capacity. After taking photographs and video footage at the bottom of the well, Dr. Starbuck made his departure for the final time, leaving the fantasies of folklore to the authority of the story teller.

As the first one-by-one meter pits were opened on various surface areas in the parade ground of the fort, it was obvious that the upper layers of soil had been largely disturbed. It was not uncommon for a time period artifact such as a military button or a musket ball to be nestled in the same soil strata as a modern day fragment of aluminum foil or a galvanized roofing nail. This was an unfortunate legacy created during the reconstruction. Large volumes of earth had been disturbed during the initial removal of the overgrowth from the property, while a good deal more of the soil was used to back fill excavation sites used during the 1950's. Due to this dismal circumstance, present day interpretations were made more perplexing, and it was not until reaching considerable depth in some of the underground rooms that typical provenience was established. ♣

One of the early discoveries in the dig was made by a jolly southern chap known as "Oklahoma Bob," a volunteer who uncovered a 1755 British half-penny while troweling in the pit at the northeast corner of the parade ground. Shortly afterward, the area outside the east curtain began producing time period artifacts. A variety of musket balls and grapeshot were unearthed, along with a fine pair of cuff links.

The site was also taking on the appearance of an 18th century refuse pit, marked by the large number of butchered animal bones and bottle fragments now predominating the overall artifact mix. The original road was never intercepted, despite extensive cross-trenching of the embankment during 1998 and 1999 under the supervision of crew chief Andy

---

♣ Provenience is a term used to indicate a strict sequential order from a given point to a point of origin, in this case a chronilogical timeline formed by successive layers of undisturbed soil.

Farry. Directly outside the southeast entrance however, Farry's crew troweled to depths in excess of nine feet, uncovering burned timbers, grape shot, musket balls, pipe stems, and miscellaneous historic artifacts. The excessive depth at which these artifacts were being discovered was at first puzzling, but it was later hypothesized that this was part of the dry moat which once wrapped around the southeast bastion and then terminated. This makes sense, since troweling a bit deeper, the artifact mix made a rather sharp transition from historic to prehistoric, characterized by Late Woodland pottery sherds, and the roasting platform mentioned in a previous chapter.

A similar transition from historic to prehistoric also became apparent as the underground casemate rooms in the parade ground of the fort were excavated to corresponding depths. The site at the northeast corner of the parade ground produced grape shot, mortar bomb fragments, and a trade axe before suffering a massive cave-in. Fortunately there were no injuries, but in the interest of safety this particular site was shut down and back filled. Future hazards of this nature were minimized by a wooden matrix of plywood and cross beams, suitably engineered by crew chief Matt Rozell to support the walls of these deep pits.

In terms of 18th century artifacts, findings on the outskirts of the property were somewhat less inspiring than those both within the fort and its immediate boundaries. The digging on these outskirts was supervised by crew chief Susan Winchell-Sweeney, who had participated in the excavations conducted by Dr. Maria Liston and Dr. Brenda Baker several years earlier on that particular area of the Fort William Henry property.

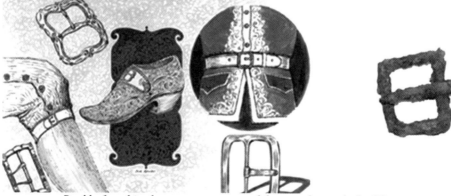

Buckle found in the casemate room of the west barracks building

At roughly 50 cm depth, plough scars were evident reflecting early farming activity during the late 18th and early 19th centuries. Various animal bones indicate the presence of livestock, while porcelain and bottle fragments dating to the late nineteenth century point to activities associated with early tourist visitation to the Fort William Henry Hotel. A series of pits was opened near the Trolley Steak House, yielding artifacts pointing to the use of that building as a Trolley station. Part of this building at one time housed an electrical AC to DC transformer complex, its existence supported by the discovery of a technologically primitive porcelain electrical insulator.

The highlight of this area was a perplexing array of retired drainage pipes having no reasonable destination. These discoveries were hardly cause for celebration, but in an archaeological context, they were in fact, part of the American historical timeline.

Below the historic layer, the artifact mix consisted chiefly of both worked and unworked chert, along with the portentous signature of Aboriginal ingenuity, the chert flake. Chert flakes were the by-product of laborious projectile point manufacture.

Aside from a three foot deep transverse utility trench dug later that season, no further digging was ever done in that area of the property. On a hot August afternoon in 1998, archaeologist John Farrell was carefully troweling around a slightly elongated dark stain in a pit which had been opened adjacent to the west barracks building at it's northern extremity. With just a few days left in the season, John was about to uncover one of the most significant discoveries of the entire project. The

The Jew's harp, a musical instrument from biblical days.

stain disappeared into the southern wall of the pit, giving the impression of a feature running almost directly parallel to the reconstructed barracks. The sudden overflow of speculation concerning the discovery was exhilarating, but with only two days remaining, sound interpretations were desperately limited.

Digging with characteristic alacrity, John dug down nearly two feet on both sides of the feature, while another one meter square pit was opened to the south. The result was an obvious formation of a partial underground log wall. Coring samples were taken indicating an artifact layer which extended considerably deeper. With time running out, the feature was covered with plastic and carefully filled in. On a note of excitement, the 1998 season came to a close.

The discovery along the west barracks building in 1998 raised questions concerning the positioning of the original fort relative to the reconstruction. Using a computer program known as CAD (Computer Aided Design), the author superimposed architectural drawings from the 1950's over original 18th century plans using the fort well as a reference point. There were no references to magnetic north on the recent drawings, but the general picture was becoming more clear. The present day east curtain wall is within one foot of the original, but the size and shape of both the southeast and northeast bastions have been skewed, probably to stay on the embankment at the time of the reconstruction. These modifications have resulted in the displacement of the entire west wall of the reconstructed fort by a distance of eight to ten feet from the position of the original structure.

Native bricks found during excavations

Envisioning the hypothetical collapse of a burning building during which all debris topples to the lowest level, the archaeology team then reasoned that the approximate ten foot construction dissimilarity might represent an artifact rich channel extending the entire length of the parade ground. Excavations over the next two successive seasons would eventu-

128

ally bear out this assumption.

    The 1999 season opened with excitement, as Matt Rozell's team immediately engaged themselves in exposing the feature which they had carefully covered over the year before. At the same time a series of pits was laid out along a projected surface line which represented the general direction of the underground feature. After troweling through a characteristic layer of modern day disturbance, time period artifacts began appearing scattered throughout a dense layer of undisturbed rubble. As the new pits were opened, various sections of the underground log structure were intersected. Thoroughly charred planks had buckled under the weight of heavy stones and crashed into the lowest floor of the building, estimated to have been 200cm below the surface of the ground. The legacy of an extremely intense fire was everywhere to be seen.

Disfigured native brick, fire cracked stone, warped brass military hard-

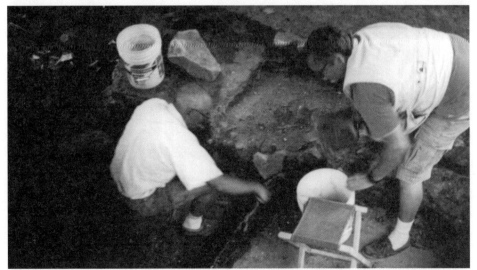

Matt Rozell and John Farrell examine casemate wall of the west barracks building

ware, and melted glass all were mixed among the rubble. Toward the bottom of the feature a number of interesting artifacts suggests significant 18th century usage of the underground room. A large number of butchered animal bones were discovered, along with lead sprew, a by-product of the musket ball molding process. These findings suggest food preparation and the passing of idle time near an open fire, possibly in a hearth. The discovery of a thimble, several lead pencils, a medicine spoon with partial cup, and a Jesuit finger ring suggests emergency medical care and possible spiritual blessing prior to death. Without further documentation however, these scenarios will forever remain in the speculative playground of imagination. Another interesting artifact found in the rubble was a Jew's Harp, a musical instrument from biblical times.

Dr. David Starbuck prepares to take photographs of the casemate feature

The feature itself also began to show signs of compartmentation, as a number of corners and cross sectional deviations from the main feature became apparent. Soon after being exposed to oxygen, wooden sections began to take on the texture of peet moss and quickly disintegrated. To facilitate the taking of photographs, this predictable decay was temporarily avoided by a periodic fine spraying with water, after which the crumbling residue was removed from the now elongated trench. The rather dark climax of the 1999 season was a miserable cave-in. There were no injuries, but six weeks of effort had become buried in a single instant. The project was not a complete exercise in futility however, since measurements and most photographs had been taken prior to the collapse. Once again the pits were filled in as the 1999 season came to a close.

Excavations along the west barracks building continued during the following season, as once again both wall and sill became perceptible in a

18ᵗʰ century grinding wheel segment and Jesuit finger ring discovered under the west barracks building

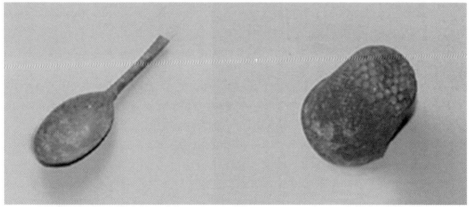

Medicine spoon and thimble also found in the west barracks casemate room

Archaeologist Charlie Brown prepares to take a depth measurement

series of carefully laid out one-meter pits. A team of volunteers headed up by crew chief John Kosec had been troweling at the approximate linear mid-point of the building where signs of another feature became apparent. With great care, both trowel and brush were used to expose the most decrepit aggregation of brick, stone, and crumbling mortar that I have ever laid eyes on, scattered in a manner so that neither chimney, hearth, nor foundation could remotely be distinguished. Butchered bone, gun flints, and nails were scattered throughout the rubble, while the overall artifact mix was not dissimilar to that of the year prior. It was not until the very bottom of the trench was reached that heavily mortared large stones took on the appearance of a hearth. The logical assumption, therefore, was that a three story chimney near the mid-point of the barracks had toppled when the building was burned approximately two hundred and fifty years ago. Once again, no human remains were found anywhere in the rubble, branding the prodigious funeral pyre so celebrated in the pages of French documents and American History books with an eternal question mark. ♣

Following a series of photographs and measurements, the pits were again filled as Dr. Starbuck's archaeology team prepared for its final departure. Archaeological work at Fort William Henry was now complete. An elongated plot along the southwest corner was left undisturbed for some future generation when there will undoubtedly exist new technologies to aid in our study of the past. The final days of 20th century Lake George have now slowly faded, and the historic soil stained with the blood of our ancestors is once again asleep. The dedicated cooperation of Archaeologists, students, and volunteers with regard to Fort William Henry and the Lake George Region has produced a sound scientific foundation to support a more clear understanding of our Early American Heritage.

♣ Some accounts describe Montcalm's troops gathering the bodies of the massacre victims and placing them on the timbers of the dismantled fort before setting fire to the wreckage. Archaeological findings do not support this.

---

[1] Historic and Prehistoric Activity at Fort William Henry   Brenda J. Baker
                                                                    Christina B. Reith 1995

Epilogue

A s the northbound stagecoach bounced along the ruts of the old military road in 1842, an interested passenger asked "What mountain is that?" "That 'ere's Frinch mounting, scene of the old Frinch war," replied the driver in a colloquial manner as destitute of eloquence as seasoned with pride. The passenger at that time was Francis Parkman, who personally visited every place he ever wrote about as an author and historian. In his many travels, Parkman never missed an opportunity to take a lexical poke at the many local inhabitants with whom he came in contact. This was his first visit to the region, and his reaction to the surroundings was not unlike many curious visitors of today. In the absence of television, billboards, and amusement parks, the "Old French War" was an exciting attraction, and one of great benefit for the Glens Falls - Lake George Stage Company. Many other travelers were also interested in the story, one that the old stage driver undoubtedly told hundreds of times. The Glens Falls - Lake George Stage Company offered what can probably be characterized as the first guided tour of the Lake George area.

As we move into the millennium, the Lake George region has more visitors than ever before, yet the overall interest in its historical significance has given way to more contemporary interests, especially among young people. This is disappointing, since so many interesting landmarks, both natural and man-made, have been named in celebration for something associated with the region's historic or pre-historic past. The most prominent is Lake George itself, and, of course, French Mountain. Others include Artillery Cove, Hatchet Island, Cooper's Cave, Fenimore Bridge, Rogers Rock, Rogers Island, and Fort Edward.

Our local streets also abound with historical names such as Montcalm, Dieskau, Uncas, Mohican, and Cooper. Roadside markers have been placed at historic locations like Bloody Pond, and monuments have been erected in memory of Sir William Johnson, Chief King Hendrick, Father Isaac Jogues, and Col. Ephram Williams.

In addition to these tributes to our Colonial heritage, a number of underwater historical preservations are maintained by an archaeological group known as "Batteaux Below." One of these preservations is a small fleet of batteaux, which was purposely sunk by the British in 1758 just off Wiawaka Point. Another is the "Land Tortise," a large armed vessel lying in approximately 100 feet of water just North of Tea Island. This site has earned a position on the National Register of Historic Landmarks. Through the efforts of "Batteaux Below," these historical sanctuaries are monitored frequently for signs of structural abnormalities or looting, ensuring their integrity for those who wish to study them.

The Lake George Steamboat Company has also maintained regional tradition with vessels suitably named "Mohican," "Minne-Ha-Ha," "Lac du St. Sacrament," and the recently decommissioned "Ticonderoga."

The tower of the old railroad station has also been restored in its original architecture, complete with four accurately attired replicas made in the likeness of a British soldier, an Indian, an American provincial, and a Ranger, all mounted on its uppermost four corners, sentries who for so long have watched over a peacetime environment that their real life predecessors could never have envisioned.

As the years pass, literally thousands of visitors travel through the Lake George region, yet only a small percentage leave with even the scant knowledge of how it derives its name. This general indifference toward our heritage, however, is not something akin to the twenty first century alone. When Francis Parkman arrived at Ticonderoga on July 26, 1842 to survey the ruins of the old fort, he was appalled at the stoicism of the inhabitants there.

134

"I asked a fellow the way to the fort." 'Well,' said he, 'I've heard of such a place, seems to me, but I never seen it, and couldn't tell ye where it be.' " You must be an idiot, thought I; but I found his case by no means singular."

"I was astonished at the extent of the ruins," says Parkman, *"All around, were ditches of such depth that it would be death to jump down, with walls of masonry sixty feet high...The senseless blockheads in the neighborhood have stolen tons upon tons of the stone to build their walls and houses of...may they meet their reward."* [1] Today, one hundred and sixty years later, the story is all too familiar.

Our Internet driven society is in no way like that to which Francis Parkman was accustomed, but that does not make our American Heritage any less significant. It is sincerely hoped that in questions and curiosities concerning their birthright, the inquisitive minority of present and future generations finds their rejoinder through the efforts of the archaeologists and historians who have spent so many hours carefully digging up history.

---

[1] The Journals of Francis Parkman   Volume I   Ref. Pg. 60

Bibliography

Handbook of North American Indians Vol. 15,
Smithsonian Institution, 1978 — William Sturtevant

A History of the Town of Queensbury
Albany, NY 1874 — A. W. Holden

Documents Relative To The Colonial History Of
The State Of New York Volume II, VI, X. — Departmente de la Guerre, Paris

The History of the Five Nations, 1866, Reprinted in
1958 by Cornell University Press — Cadwallader Colden

New York State Historical Society
MDCCCCXXIII 1921 — Departmente de la Guerre, Paris

The Great War for the Empire
New York, 1946 — Lawrence Henry Gibson

The Jesuits in North America
Boston, 1902 — Francis Parkman

New York State Historical Association, Volume XX
New York, 1922

Aboriginal Settlement Patterns in the Northeast
New York State Museum, 1973 — Ritchie, Funk

136

New York State Projectile Points, Bulletin 384
Revised 1971, Reprinted 1997 — William Ritchie

The Diary of Jabez Fitch in the French and Indian War
in 1757, Second Edition 1968 — Rogers Island Historical Association

The Diary and Journal of Seth Metcalf (1755-1807)
Boston, 1939 — Worcester Historical Society

Montcalm and Wolfe
New York, 1984 — Francis Parkman

The Journals and Papers of Seth Pomeroy
New York, 1826 — The Society of Colonial Wars

Guide to the Geology of the Lake George Region
Albany, NY, 1942 — D. H. Newland

Canadian Archives, Ref 5·47 5·48 — Departmente de la Guerre, Paris

The Diary of Rev. Samuel Chandler
Gloucester, MA, 1863 — New England Historical and Genealogical Register

Fort William Henry, A History
Lake George, NY, 1955 — Stanley M. Gifford

Chronicles of Lake George
New York, 1995 — Russell P. Bellico

Indian History of New York State, The Iroquoian Tribes
Educational Leaflet Series #7, Part II. — William Ritchie

The French and Indian Wars
New York, 1962 — Francis P. Russell

Carver's Travels
Minneapolis, 1778 — Jonathan Carver

The Journals of Francis Parkman, Volume I 1947 — Massachusetts Historical Society

The History of Fort George
New York, 1871 — B.F. Decosta

137

Digging up History

Trauma in Eighteenth Century Military Remains at Fort William Henry, 1995	Dr. Maria Liston Dr. Brenda Baker
Relief is Greatly Wanted New York, 1998	Edward J. Dodge
Betrayals New York, 1990	Ian Steele
New England Indians Connecticut, 1978	C. Keith Wilbur
Prehistoric Archaeology, Leaflet #22	New York State Museum Albany, NY
William Johnson Papers, Volume II	New York State Museum Albany, NY
Reconstructing the Massacre at Fort William Henry 1995	Dr. Maria Liston Dr. Brenda Baker
The History of Rogers Rangers San Francisco, 1946	Burt B. Loescher
Lake George, A Book of Today New York, 1884	S. R. Stoddard
The History of the State of New York New York, 1831	A. K. White
A Historical Journal of the Campaigns In North America by Capt. John Knox, Volume I Toronto, 1914	The Champlain Society
Revolutionary Medicine 1700- 1800 Library of Congress #80-82790 1980	C. Keith Wilbur